Souad now lives in Europe. She is married with three children.

BURNED ALIVE

Souad

in collaboration with
Marie-Thérèse Cuny

Translated from the French
by Judith S. Armbruster

BANTAM BOOKS

LONDON • TORONTO • SYDNEY • AUCKLAND • JOHANNESBURG

BURNED ALIVE
A BANTAM BOOK : 9780553816303
0553816306

Originally published in Great Britain by Bantam Press,
a division of Transworld Publishers

PRINTING HISTORY
Bantam Press edition published 2004
Bantam edition published 2005

7 9 10 8 6

Set in 12.5/16pt Bembo by
Falcon Oast Graphic Art Ltd.

Bantam Books are published by Transworld Publishers,
61–63 Uxbridge Road, London W5 5SA,
a division of The Random House Group Ltd,
in Australia by Random House Australia (Pty) Ltd,
20 Alfred Street, Milsons Point, Sydney, NSW 2061, Australia,
in New Zealand by Random House New Zealand Ltd,
18 Poland Road, Glenfield, Auckland 10, New Zealand
and in South Africa by Random House (Pty) Ltd, Isle of Houghton,
Corner Boundary Road & Carse O'Gowrie, Houghton 2198, South Africa.

Printed and bound in Great Britain by
Cox & Wyman Ltd, Reading, Berkshire.

Papers used by Transworld Publishers are natural, recyclable
products made from wood grown in sustainable forests. The
manufacturing processes conform to the environmental
regulations of the country of origin.

CONTENTS

Part I

Souad

I WAS IN FLAMES

I am a girl. A girl must walk fast, head down, as if counting the number of steps she's taking. She may never stray from her path or look up, for if a man catches her eye, the whole village labels her a *charmuta*. If a married neighbour woman, or an old woman, or just anybody sees her out without her mother or her older sister, without her sheep, her bundle of hay or her load of figs, they say, '*Charmuta*.' A girl must be married before she can raise her eyes and look straight ahead, or go into a shop, or pluck her eyebrows and wear jewellery. My mother was married at fourteen. If a girl is still unmarried by that age, the village begins to make fun of her. But a girl must wait her turn in the family to be married. The eldest daughter first, then the others.

There were too many girls in my father's house, four of marrying age at the same time. There were also two half-sisters, born of our father's second wife, who were still children. The one male child of the family, the son who was adored by all, was our brother Assad, who was born in glory among all these daughters. He was the fourth born. I was the third.

Adnan, my father, was not pleased with my mother, Leila, for giving him all these girls. He was unhappy, too, with his other wife, Aicha, who had also produced only girls. Noura, the eldest daughter, was married late, when I was about fifteen. Nobody asked for Kainat, the second, who was about a year older than me. I overheard that a man had spoken to my father about me, but he was told that I must wait for Kainat's marriage before I could marry. But perhaps Kainat was not pretty enough, and probably too slow at her work. I'm still not sure why she wasn't asked for, but if she stayed unmarried, she'd be the butt of the village jokes, and so would I.

It is a curse in my village to be born a girl: I have no memory of having played games or having fun as a child – the only freedom a girl can dream about is marriage, leaving your father's house for your husband's and not coming back, even if you're beaten. It is considered shameful for a married daughter to return home because she is not supposed to ask for protection outside her husband's house. If she does return to her father's house, it is her family's duty to take her back to her husband. My sister was beaten by her husband and she brought shame on our family when she came home to complain.

She was lucky to have a husband, though. I dreamed about it. As soon as I heard that a man had spoken to my father about me, I was consumed with impatience and curiosity. I knew he lived three or four steps from us. Sometimes I caught sight of him from the upper terrace where I laid out the laundry to dry. He must have had a good job in the city because he didn't dress like a labourer. He always wore a suit, carried a briefcase, and had a car. I'd have liked to see his face close up but I was afraid the family would catch me spying. So, when I went to get hay for a sick sheep in the stable, I walked fast, hoping to see him nearby. But he parked his car too far away. From watching, I knew what time he came out to go to work, and at seven o'clock in the morning, I'd pretend to be fold- ing the laundry on the terrace, or looking for a ripe fig, or shaking out the carpets so that I could glimpse him driving off in his car. I had to be quick so I wasn't noticed. I used to climb the stairs and pass through the rooms to get to the terrace. There I shook a rug energetically and looked over the cement wall, just glancing to the right. If somebody had noticed me from a distance, they wouldn't have guessed that I was looking down at the street.

When I saw him, I realized I was in love with him — and his car! I imagined many things on the terrace — that I was married to him and watching the car drive away until I couldn't see it any more. But he'd come back from work at sunset and I'd remove his shoes and, on my knees, I'd wash his feet as my mother did for my father. I would bring him tea, and watch him smoke his long pipe, seated like a king before the front door of his house. I would be a woman with a husband! And maybe I'd even be able to put on makeup, get into the car with him, and go into town to the shops. I would endure anything for the simple freedom of being able to go out to buy bread! But I would never be a *charmuta*. I would not look at other men. I would continue to walk fast, erect and proud, but I would no longer watch my steps with lowered eyes, and the village would not say bad things about me because I would be a married woman.

It was on that terrace that my terrible story began. By then I was already older than my sister Noura was on her wedding day. I must have been eighteen, maybe more, I don't know, and I both hoped and despaired. My memory went up in smoke the day the flames engulfed me but I have tried to reconstruct what happened.

MEMORY

I was born in a tiny village, which, I'm told, was somewhere in the West Bank. Since I never went to school, I learnt nothing of my country's history. I have also been told that I was born there either in 1957 or 1958, so I'm about forty-five today. Twenty-five years ago, I spoke only Arabic; I'd hardly been further than a few kilometres beyond the last house on the dirt road. I knew there were cities further away but I had never seen them. I did not know if the earth was round or flat, and I had no idea of the world. What I did know was that we had to hate the Jews, who had taken our land; my father called them pigs. We were forbidden to go near them for fear of becoming pigs like them.

I had to say my prayers at least twice a day. I recited them like my mother and sisters, but I only learnt of the Qur'ān in Europe many years later. My only brother, treated like the king of the house, went to school, but the girls did not. As I've already said, where I come from, being born a girl is a curse: a wife must first produce a son, at least one, and if she gives birth to only girls, she is mocked. At most, two or three girls are needed to help with the housework, to work on the land and tend the animals. If more girls are born, it is a great misfortune and they should be got rid of as soon as possible. I lived like this until I was about eighteen, knowing nothing except that I was worth less than an animal because I was a girl.

So, this was my first life, as an Arab woman in the West Bank. It lasted nearly twenty years, and the person I had been there died. She is no more.

My second life began in Europe at the end of the 1970s in an international airport. I was not

Eat? Sleep? Walk?' I answered by making signs for yes or no. Much later I learnt to read words in a newspaper, patiently, day after day. In the beginning I could decipher only short announcements, death notices, or short sentences with a few words that I would repeat phonetically. Sometimes I felt like an animal who was being taught to communicate as a human. In my head, in Arabic, I asked myself where I was, in what country, and why I hadn't died in my village. I was ashamed to be alive still, although no one knew this. I was afraid of my new life but no one understood.

I remember little of my earliest childhood and my memory is still full of gaps. The first part of my life is made up of images that are strange and violent, like scenes in a film. I have so much difficulty putting them in order that it sometimes doesn't seem real. For example, how could I forget the name of one of my sisters, or my brother's age on the day of his wedding, yet remember everything about the goats, the lambs, the cows, the bread oven, the laundry in the garden, about picking the cauliflowers, the and wash my pants secretly to make them white again, then dry them quickly in the sun so the men and the neighbours wouldn't see them. Two pairs were all I had. I used paper for protection on those awful days when I was considered to have the plague. I buried it, the sign of my impurity, in secret in the rubbish pail. If I had cramps, my mother boiled sage leaves and gave the infusion to me to drink. She wrapped my head tightly in a scarf and the next day I had no more pain. It is the only medicine I remember and I still use it because it works.

In the early mornings I went to the stable where I whistled, using my fingers, for the sheep to gather round me, then left for the pasture with my sister Kainat, the one who was about a year older than me. Girls are not to go out alone but should be accompanied by someone older: the elder serves as safeguard for the younger. My sister Kainat was round and a little chubby, while I was small and thin. We got along well. The two of us went with the sheep and goats to the field, about a quarter of an hour's walk from the village, walking fast, eyes lowered, as far as the last house. Once we were in the field, we were free to say silly things to each other and even laugh a little but I don't remember any of our conversations. We ate our cheese, feasted on watermelon, and watched the sheep and, especially, the goats, which were capable of devouring all the leaves of a fig tree in a few minutes. When the sheep moved into a circle to sleep, we fell asleep in the shade – which was risky: an animal might have wandered into a neighbouring field, and we would then have to suffer the consequences when we got home. If it destroyed a vegetable garden or we were a few minutes late getting back to the stable, we were thrashed with a belt.

I had to shear the sheep, too. I would take each animal by its hoofs, get it to lie down on the ground, then tie it up and clip the wool with the shears. They were so big for my small hands that after only a few minutes I had trouble using them. I sat on the ground or on a stool to milk the ewes, their hoofs squeezed between my legs. We used the milk to make cheese, or when it had cooled, we drank it.

Our village was very pretty and green. Many fruits grew there, figs, grapes, lemons, and an enormous number of olive trees. My father owned half of the cultivated parcels of the village. He wasn't very rich but he had possessions. Our stone house was big, and surrounded by a wall with a large door of grey iron. This door was the symbol of our captivity. Once we were inside, it closed on us to prevent us going out. You could enter by this door from the outside, but you could not go out again.

Was there a key or an automatic system? My father and mother went out, but not we girls. My brother was as free as the wind. He went out and came back through that door; he went to the movies – he did as he liked. I often looked at that iron door, and said to myself, 'I'll never be able to leave through there, never . . .'

I didn't have a good sense of the village because I couldn't go out when and where I pleased. Now if I close my eyes and make an effort, I can remember what I saw of it. There was my parents' house, then the one I called the rich people's house a little further along on the same side. Opposite was the house of my beloved, which I could see from the terrace. You crossed the road and there it was. There were a few other scattered houses, but I don't know how many – very few. They were surrounded by low walls or iron fences and the owners had vegetable gardens like us. I never went the entire length of the village. I only left the house to go to market with my father and mother, or to the fields with my sister and the animals. That was all.

Until I was seventeen or eighteen, I had seen nothing else. I had not set foot in the shop near our house in the village, but when I passed by in my father's van to go to market, I would always see the merchant standing at his door smoking his cigarettes. The shop had separate entrances for men and women. The men used the one on the right to go in and buy their cigarettes, newspapers and drinks, and on the left the women chose their fruit and vegetables. In another house on the same side of the road as ours a married woman lived with four children. She had the right to go out to the shop. I remember her standing by the fruit and vegetables holding transparent plastic bags.

There was a lot of land around our house, which was full of vegetables we had planted, squash, cauliflower and tomatoes, and fruit. Grapes grew along the terrace, where I picked them. There were oranges, bananas, too, and lots of black and green figs – a memory I'll never lose is of going out early in the mornings to pick the figs which had opened a little in the coolness of the night: the juice would run like honey. Our garden was separated from the garden of the neighbouring house by a low wall that you could step over, although none of us ever did. Being closed in was normal. It would never have occurred to any of the girls of the house to cross this symbolic barrier. In the village or on the road, a girl alone would have been spotted quickly and her reputation destroyed with the family's honour.

It was in this garden that I did the laundry. There was a well in one corner, and I heated the water in a basin over a wood fire. I would take a bundle of kindling from the woodpile and mother, my sisters and me. When it was time to gather the figs, we would set out even earlier: they had to be picked one by one, then put into crates and my father would take them to market. It was a good half-hour's walk with the donkey to a small town whose name I've forgotten, if I ever knew it. Half of the market at the town's entrance was reserved for produce and the merchants who were there to sell it. To shop for clothes, you took the bus to a larger town. But we girls never went there. My mother went with my father. It was like this: she'd buy a dress with my father and then she'd give it to one of us. Whether you liked it or not, you had to wear it. It was that dress or nothing.

Girls wore long dresses with short sleeves made of a type of cotton, a warm material that pricked your skin. They were grey, usually, or sometimes white, very rarely black. The collar was high and tightly fastened. Over this we had to put on a long-sleeved shirt or a vest, according to the season. It was sometimes so hot that it was stifling, but it had to have long sleeves. To show a bit of arm or leg or, worse, any skin below the neck, brought shame. Under the long dress we wore the *saroual*, long baggy pants, either grey or white, then a pair of underpants, cut big like shorts, that reached above the stomach. All my sisters dressed like this. Usually women did not wear shoes, except sometimes married women – my mother went barefoot – so when we went into the fields, we got thorns in our feet and had to sit down to pull them out.

We had little contact with other girls in the village, except at weddings. Then our conversations were banal, about the food, about the bride, about other girls' looks, or maybe about a woman we thought lucky because she was wearing makeup.

'Look at that one, she's plucked her eyebrows!'

'She has a nice haircut.'

'Oh, she's wearing *shoes*!' (The richest girl in the village wore embroidered slippers.)

My mother was often dressed in black. My father wore a white *saroual*, a long shirt and the traditional red and white headscarf. My father! I can see him now, sitting under a tree on the

ground in front of our house, his cane nearby:
he had a pale complexion with red splotches, a
round head and mean blue eyes. One day he
broke his leg in a fall from a horse and we girls
were so pleased: it meant he couldn't run after
us as fast as before to beat us with his belt.

I see him very clearly. I can never forget him.
It is as if I carry a photograph of him in my
head. He is sitting in front of his house like a
king before his palace, with his red and white
scarf that covers his bald red skull; he's wearing
his belt and his cane rests on the leg folded
under him.

He was small and mean. He would take off
his belt and shout, 'Why have the sheep come
back by themselves?' then pull me by the hair
and drag me into the kitchen. He struck me
once while I was kneeling, pulled my hair as if
he wanted to pull it out and cut it off with the
big scissors used for shearing the sheep. I had
hardly any hair left. I could cry, yell or plead but
he would only continue to hit me. It really was
my fault about the sheep – I had fallen asleep
with my sister because it was so hot, and I let the

sheep go off on their own. He'd hit me so hard with his cane that sometimes I couldn't lie down on either my left or right side because I was in so much pain. I think we were beaten every day with the belt or the cane. A day without a beating was unusual. Once he tied us up, Kainat and me, our hands behind our backs, our legs bound, and a scarf over our mouths to stop us screaming. We stayed like that all night, tied to a gate in the stable. We were with the animals, but worse off than they were.

This was what it was like in our village. It was the law of men. The girls and women were beaten every day in the other houses, too. You could hear the crying. It was not unusual to be beaten, or to have your hair shaved and be tied to a stable gate. There was no other way of living.

My father was all-powerful, the king of the household, who owned, who decided, who hit and tortured us. And he sat there calmly smoking his pipe in front of his house with his women, whom he treated worse than his livestock, locked up. In my country a man takes a woman to have sons and serve him as a slave, like the daughters who will come, if she has the misfortune to produce any.

When I looked at my brother, who was adored by the whole family, including me, I often thought, What makes him so special? He came out of the same belly as I did. But that was just the way it was. We girls had to serve him as we did my father, grovelling, with head lowered. I can also picture the tea tray. We had to bring it to the men of the family with our heads down, looking only at our feet, back bent, and in silence. You didn't speak, except in answer to a question.

In the morning I made tea for the girls. I heated the water in a basin on the coals of the bread oven. The dried green tea leaves were in a sack of tan cloth on the floor in a corner of the kitchen. I plunged my hand into it, took out a handful and put it into the teapot. I knew that if I dropped any on the floor, I would be beaten. So I paid attention. If I was clumsy, I shouldn't sweep it up, but rather pick it up and put it back in the teapot. I added sugar, then returned to the garden for the hot water. The basin was heavy and I had to carry it by its two handles, with my back arched so I did not burn myself. I came back into the kitchen and poured the water into the teapot, slowly, over the tea and the sugar. Then my sisters came in, but I can't remember my father, mother and brother ever being with us for breakfast or how old I was at this time — I do know that the eldest, Noura, wasn't married yet. At noon, it was sugared rice, vegetables with chicken or mutton, and bread. In my father's house, the garden gave us almost everything we needed for food. And we did everything ourselves. My father bought only sugar, salt and tea. There was always food to eat — the family lacked nothing for meals.

I must have been about fifteen when Noura married. My sister Kainat was still at home, not married. I had a younger sister, too, whose name escapes me — even now when I try to remember it, it won't come to me. I'll call her Hanan, but may she forgive me because it surely wasn't her name. I know she took care of the two little half-sisters my father brought home after he abandoned his second wife, Aicha. He always wanted sons, and when my mother failed to give him one, it was accepted that he would find another wife. But Aicha failed him too: she gave him only two more girls, so he dropped her and brought the two new little sisters home to us. That was considered normal too – everything a man wanted to do was considered normal in our village, and at that time I couldn't imagine any other kind of life. I didn't imagine anything at all. In our childhood, we knew no play or toys, no games, only obedience and submission.

Anyway, the two little girls came to live with us and Hanan stayed at home to take care of them – I'm sure of that. In my first memories of them, they are five or six, too young to work. In our family, the children were about a year apart. My mother was married at fourteen, and my father was much older. She had many children – fourteen in all – but only five survived. One day while I served the tea my mother's father said, and I can still hear his words in my ears: 'It's good that you married young, you were able to have fourteen children . . . and a son. It's very good.' Although I didn't go to school, I knew how to count the sheep – so I could count on my fingers that there were only five of us, Noura, Kainat, Souad, Assad and Hanan. Where were the others? My mother did not say directly that they had died. 'I have fourteen children, seven of them are living.' She included the half-sisters with us five – we never referred to them as 'half-sisters,' always 'sisters'. So, it might seem that seven were missing. But if you didn't count the half-sisters, it was nine. Either way, many of the children she had borne were dead.

One day I learnt why there were only seven of us in the house. I can't say how old I was, but I hadn't reached puberty, so I must have been less than ten, and Noura was with me. I have forgotten many things, but not this, which I saw with my own eyes. I was terrified, but I didn't know that what I witnessed was a crime.

My mother was lying on the floor on a

sheepskin. She was giving birth, and my aunt Salima was with her sitting on a cushion. There were cries from my mother and then from the baby. Very quickly my mother took the sheepskin and smothered the baby. I saw the baby move once and then it was over. I don't remember what happened after that, just that the baby wasn't there any more. She was a girl. I saw my mother do it this first time, then a second time. I'm not sure I was present for the third, but I knew about it. And I heard Noura say to her: 'If I have girls, I'll do what you have done.'

That was how my mother got rid of the seven girls she had after Hanan, the last survivor. In our village it was accepted as normal – and I accepted it, too, but I was frightened: these little girls my mother had killed were part of me. From then on I hid and cried every time my father killed a sheep or a chicken. To my parents the death of an animal, or a baby, was an everyday event, but now I feared that I might disappear as simply and quickly as the babies had. I would tell myself that it would be my turn one day, or my sister's. They could kill us whenever they wanted to. Big or small, there was no difference. Since they had given us life, they had the right to take it.

As long as I lived with my parents, I feared I would die suddenly. I was afraid of going up a ladder when my father was below. I was afraid of the hatchet used for chopping the wood, afraid of the well when I went for water. I was afraid when my father watched the sheep returning to the stable with us, and afraid of being suffocated under the sheepskin that was my bed.

Sometimes, coming back from the fields with the animals, Kainat and I talked about it: 'Supposing everybody's dead when we get home . . . And what if Father has killed Mother? A blow with a stone is all it would take! What would we do?'

'Every time I go to the well I pray because it's so deep. I tell myself that if somebody pushed me in, no one would know where I was. You could die down there – nobody would come looking for you.'

That well was my greatest terror, and my mother's, too. I sensed it. And I was afraid of the ravines when I led the goats and the sheep home. The idea would loom up in me that my father might be hiding somewhere and that he would push me into the void. It would be easy for him to do. When they found me, they would pile a few stones over me and I would be left there to rot.

The possibility of our mother dying pre-occupied us more than the death of a sister because there were always other sisters. Our mother was often beaten, just as we were. Sometimes she tried to intervene when my father hit us especially viciously, and then he'd turn on her, knocking her down and pulling her hair. We lived every day with the possibility of death. It could come for no reason, take you by surprise, simply because Father had decided you should die. Just as my mother had decided to smother the baby girls. She would be pregnant, then she wasn't, and nobody asked any questions. I never knew what became of the baby girls after my mother smothered them. Did they bury them somewhere? Did they become food for the dogs? Every birth of a girl was like a burial in the family. My mother would dress in black, my father also. It was always considered the mother's fault if she produced only girls. My father thought so and so did the whole village.

If a woman gave birth to a son, and he was alive, then glory to her and to the family. If he was dead, everyone wept over him and the misfortune that had befallen the family. The males counted, not the females.

In my village, if the men had to choose between a girl and a cow, they would choose the cow. My father repeated endlessly how we girls were good for nothing. A cow produces milk and calves. What do you do with milk and calves? You sell them and bring the money home. But a girl? What does the family get from her? Nothing. What do sheep bring to us? Wool. You sell the wool and you get money. Their lambs grow up, produce more lambs, more milk, you make cheese, you sell it and bring home money. A cow and a sheep are more valuable than a girl. And we girls knew this because the cows, the sheep and the goats were never beaten.

We knew, too, that a girl is a problem for her father because he is always afraid that he will not be able to marry her off – then again, if she's married and her husband mistreats her, her family is shamed if she leaves him and dares to return to her parents' house. But as long as she is not married, the father is afraid that she'll become an old maid and the village will gossip. For the whole family that is a terrible embarrassment: if an unmarried girl walks in the street with her father and mother, everyone makes fun of her. It is not normal for her still to be in her parents' house when she is twenty. A girl is expected to be married. I don't know how this worked in the big cities of my country but that is the way it was in my village.

HANAN

My sisters and I had an abiding fear of death and of the iron door. My brother Assad, though, would leave for school with a satchel. He went horse-riding, too, and walking. He did not eat with us. He grew up as a man should, free and proud, and was served like a prince by the girls of the house. Assad was handsome and I adored him. I heated the water for his bath when he was small and washed his hair. I took care of him as you would a priceless treasure. I knew nothing of his life outside the house and I was ignorant of what he learnt at school, and of what he saw and did in town.

There was only a year between us, which

meant I could be close to him while he was still a child. I don't have any memory of playing with him as children of that age do in Europe, and by the age of fourteen or fifteen he was a man and had drifted away from me.

I think he married young, probably when he was seventeen. He had also become violent. My father hated him, but I did not know why. Perhaps Assad was too much like him, and he was afraid of losing his power to a son who had become an adult. I don't know the origin of the anger between them, but one day I saw my father take a basket and fill it with stones, then go up on the terrace and hurl them at Assad's head, as if he wanted to kill him.

When he married, Assad lived with his wife in a part of our house. He pushed an armoire against the connecting door to keep my father out. I soon understood that the violence of the men of my village comes from way back in our history: a father passes it to his son who transmits it in his turn.

I haven't seen my family for twenty-five years, but if by some chance I were to come across my brother, I would like to ask him just one question: 'Where is our sister Hanan, who disappeared?' Hanan — I can see her — was a beautiful girl, very dark and prettier than me, with thick hair and heavy eyebrows that joined above her eyes. I remember that Kainat was sweet and good, but a little too heavy, and that Hanan was a little abrupt in her manner, but submissive like the rest of us. She was not fat but you sensed that she might become strong and chubby. She was not thin like me. When she came to help us pick olives, she worked and moved slowly. This wasn't usual in my family: you walked fast, you worked fast, you ran to bring out the animals. Rather than being active, she was dreamy and never very attentive to what was said to her. When we were picking olives, my fingers would be sore from having collected a bowlful but she wouldn't have covered the bottom of hers. I would help her because if she was behind everyone else my father would beat her.

Now I can see us all in a row in the olive grove: we go forward in a line, stooped and moving with the rhythm of the picking. As soon as a hand is full, we throw the olives into the bowl and keep going until the bowl is almost overflowing, then tip them into the big cloth sacks. Each time I come back to my place, I see that Hanan is still behind, as if she is moving in slow motion. I have no recollection of talking to her or of being much involved with her, except for helping her with the olive picking – or twisting her thick hair into a plait, as she was supposed to do for me. I don't see her with us in the stable or leading the cows, or shearing the sheep. She spent most of her time in the kitchen helping my mother, which may be why she has almost disappeared from my memory. For years I didn't wonder about her disappearance from my family. I forgot her, as if a door had closed on her, making her invisible to my memory, which was already jumbled.

Some time ago, however, a brutal image arose in my mind. Someone, in a gathering of women, showed me a photo of a dead girl who had been strangled with a black telephone cord. I had a feeling I had seen something similar before. The photo made me uneasy, not only because of this unfortunate murdered girl but because I was groping to 'see' something that concerned me. The next day my memory returned with a shock. I knew I had witnessed this scene. Now I remembered when and how my sister Hanan had disappeared.

Since that moment of recognition I have lived with this new nightmare in my head. Every scene that returns of my past life makes me feel sick. I would like to forget it completely, and for more than twenty years I succeeded in doing just that. But to bear witness to my life as child and woman in my country, I am forced to immerse myself in memories like this one. And all the bits of my past that rise to the surface seem now so appalling that I can hardly bring myself to believe them.

When I'm alone, I sometimes ask myself if I really lived through these things. I am still here, I survived them. Other women have lived through these things and they, too, are still in the world. But we survivors who can speak out are so few that it is my duty to bear witness, and to do that I must relive the nightmares.

As for Hanan, I was in the house when I heard shouting. I ran to see what was happening. My sister was sitting on the floor, arms and legs flailing, and Assad was leaning over her, strangling her with the telephone cord. I remember this scene as if it took place yesterday. I was standing in front of my two little sisters to shield them. We pressed ourselves against the wall to try to make ourselves disappear. I held them by the hair so that they couldn't move. Assad must have seen us or heard me come in, because he yelled: '*Rouhi! Rouhi!* Get out! Get out!'

I ran to the cement stairs that led to the bedrooms dragging my little sisters. One was so afraid that she stumbled and hurt her leg, but I made her keep going. My whole body was trembling as I locked us in the room, then consoled her. We stayed there for a long time, the three of us, not making a sound. I could do nothing, absolutely nothing, but keep quiet, with this vision of horror in my head of my brother strangling our sister. She must have been using the telephone and he came up behind to strangle her. That day she was wearing white trousers, with a shirt that went to the knees. I saw her legs kick and I saw her arms strike my brother in the face as he shouted at me, 'Get out!'

The telephone was black, I think. How long had it been in the house? There couldn't have been many in the village at that time. It had arrived when my father modernized our house. It was kept on the floor in the main room and had a very long cord. Hanan must have been trying to use it, but I don't know whom she was calling or why. I don't know what I was doing before that, or where I was, or what Hanan might have been doing, but nothing could have justified my brother strangling her.

I stayed in the bedroom with the little girls until my mother came back. She and my father had gone out with my sister Noura, leaving us alone with Assad. That day, my parents had gone to see my brother's wife at her parents' house, where she had taken refuge because she was pregnant and Assad had beaten her. That was why my brother was alone with us in our house. And he must have been furious, like all men, to be insulted like this. As usual, I had only snatches of information about what was happening – a girl is not present at family meetings when there are conflicts: she's kept out of the way. I learnt later that my sister-in-law had had a miscarriage, and I suppose my parents and perhaps hers, too, had accused my brother of being responsible for it.

What was Hanan doing on the telephone? It was used very little. I had used it only a few times to speak to my older sister, my aunt or my brother's wife. If Hanan had been calling someone, it must have been a family member.

When my parents came home, my mother spoke to Assad. I saw her crying, but I know now she was just pretending: I've come to understand how things happen in my land. I know why they kill girls and how it happens. It is decided at a family meeting and on the fatal day the parents are never present. Only the one who has been chosen to do the killing is with the intended victim.

My mother wasn't really crying. She knew why my brother had strangled my sister. If not, why had she gone out that day with my father and Noura? Why leave me and the little ones alone in the house with Assad? I don't know why Hanan was condemned to die. She must have committed a sin but I have no idea what it was. Did she go out alone? Was she seen speaking to a man? Was she denounced by a neighbour? It doesn't take much for everyone to see a girl as a *charmuta* who has brought shame to the family and must die to restore the honour of her parents and brother – of the entire village, even.

My sister was more mature than I, even if she was younger in age. She must have committed an imprudence that I wasn't aware of. Girls don't exchange confidences. They're too afraid of speaking, even among sisters. I know something about this, because I also kept silent.

I loved my brother very much. We all loved him because he was the only man of the family after my father. If Father had died, he would have run the home, and if he died, and only the women were left, the family would have been lost. No more sheep, no more land, no more anything. Losing an only son and brother is the worst thing that can happen to a family. How can you live without a man? It is the man who makes the law and protects us; it is the son who takes the place of the father and marries off his sisters.

As I have said, Assad was violent like my father. He was a murderer, but in my village that word has no meaning when a woman is killed. It is the duty of the brother, the brother-in-law or the uncle to preserve the family's honour. If the father or mother says to her son, 'Your sister has sinned, you must kill her,' he does it for the sake of honour and because it is the law.

Still, today, I can't fully accept that Assad is a murderer. The image of my strangled sister is a recurring nightmare now, but at the time I don't think I held it against him: what he did was the accepted custom. He must have agreed to do it out of duty. And, anyway, I loved him.

I don't know what they did with Hanan's body but it disappeared from the house. I forgot about her but I don't understand why. Besides fear, there is, of course, the logic of my life at that time, the customs, the law, everything that made us live with these things as though they were normal. They were only crimes and horrors elsewhere, like in the West, or in other countries where the laws are different. I was supposed to die too. And I survived the customary punishment of my land by a miracle. Now I can see that the shock of what happened to me made me 'forget' other events in my life. At least, that's what a psychiatrist told me.

So that was how Hanan disappeared from my life and from my memory for a long time. Maybe she was buried with the babies. Maybe they burned her or buried her under a pile of debris or in a field. Perhaps they gave her to the dogs. I don't know. When I talk about my life there, I can see from people's expressions the difficulty they have in understanding. They ask me questions that seem logical to them: 'Did the police come?' 'Wasn't anyone concerned about a person's disappearance?' 'What did the people in the village say?'

I never saw the police – it's nothing if a woman disappears. And the village people agree with the men's law: if you don't kill a girl who has dishonoured her family, villagers will reject the family, and nobody will speak to them or do business with them. They have to leave.

Now I can see that my sister's fate was worse than mine. But at least she isn't suffering now – she is dead. I still hear her cries in my ears – she screamed so loudly. Kainat and I were afraid for a long time. Every time we saw my father, my brother or my brother-in-law, we were afraid they would do something to us. Sometimes we couldn't sleep. I woke up frequently at night. I felt a permanent threat over me.

Assad was always angry and violent. For a time he wasn't allowed to see his wife. She had gone to her parents' house when she left hospital because he had beaten her so severely. Later she returned to live with him – it's the law. She gave him other children, fortunately sons. We were proud of him, we loved him so much, even if he frightened us. I don't understand why I adored my brother yet hated my father: in the end they were alike.

If I had got married in my village, and given birth to girls, Assad might have been ordered to strangle one. Like all the other women, I would have submitted to this. I would not have rebelled. It's unbearable to think such a thing now, in my new life, but that is the way it was. Now I see things very differently because I 'died' in my village and was reborn in Europe. But my love for my brother is like the root of an olive tree that can't be torn out, even if the tree has fallen.

THE GREEN TOMATO

Every morning I cleaned out the stable. It was very large and the stench was overpowering. When I had finished, I would leave the door open to air it. It was damp and, with the heat of the sun, soon steamy too. Then I carried the buckets of manure on my head into the garden to dry. Some of it, from the horses, was used in the garden. My father said it was the best fertilizer. The sheep droppings were used for the bread oven: when they were thoroughly dry I would sit on the ground and work them by hand into little cakes.

When we returned from the fields at around eleven o'clock when the sun was strong, I went into the house to eat, some oil in a bowl, warm bread, olives and fruit, with tea.

During the heat of the day, I worked in the house. I prepared the dough for the bread and fed the smallest lambs. I would take them by the scruff of the neck, the way you pick up a cat, and hold them up to the ewe's udder. When one had finished I would continue with the next until they had all been fed. Then I would go to the goats. The stable held a good sixty sheep and at least forty goats; the two horses had their own corner and the cows, too. The horses were in the fields during the day, and came in only at night. They were for my father and brother to ride, never us. When the stable work was finished, I could leave the door open for ventilation because a heavy wooden gate kept the animals inside.

When the sun was lower in the sky, I tended the garden. In season, the tomatoes had to be picked almost every day as they ripened. Once, by mistake, I picked a green tomato. I haven't forgotten that tomato. I often think about it now. It was half yellow and half red, just beginning to ripen. I thought about hiding it when I brought it into the house, but it was too late: my father was there. I knew I shouldn't have picked it but I was working too fast with both hands. My movements were mechanical: my fingers flew round the tomato plant, left, right, left, right, down to the bottom. And the last one, the one that had received the least sun, was in my hand before I knew it. And now it was in the basin. 'You fool!' my father shouted. 'You see what you've done? You've picked a green tomato! *Majmouma!*' He struck me, and then he crushed the tomato on my head so that the seeds fell over me. 'Now you're going to eat it!' He crammed as much as he could into my mouth, then rubbed the rest over my face.

I'd thought that an unripe tomato might taste all right, but it was very sour and smelled horrible. He made me swallow it. I didn't want to eat anything after that because I felt ill, but my father pushed my head into my plate and made me eat my meal like a dog. He had me by the hair and I couldn't move. My little sister made fun of me and laughed. She received such the goats back to the fields and stayed until sunset. My sister walked at the head of the flock and I at the rear with a cane to move the animals along. The goats were always excited, ready to take off. When we got to the field, there was a little peace because it was only us and the flock. Sometimes I would take a watermelon with me and tap it on a stone to open it. We were afraid of being found out when we returned because our dresses were spotted with the juice. We would wash them on ourselves in the stable before our parents saw us. We couldn't take them off so it was lucky that they dried fast. By then, the sun was fading on the horizon, the sky changing from blue to grey. We had to return before nightfall, and since night comes quickly in my country, we had to move as fast as the sun, scurrying close to the walls – and then the iron door would clang shut on us again.

When it was time to milk the cows and sheep, a big milk can was put under the animal's belly, and I sat on a stool almost at ground level. I would take a hoof and squeeze it between my legs so that the animal couldn't move and the she tried to question me he hit her too. He told her it wasn't any of her business, that she didn't need to know why I'd been beaten because I knew the reason.

On an ordinary day, he would slap or kick me because I wasn't working fast enough or the water for the tea had taken too long to boil. Sometimes I succeeded in dodging a blow but not often. I don't remember if my sister Kainat was beaten as much as I was, but I think she must have been because she was every bit as afraid as I was. To this day I work and walk fast, as if a belt were permanently waiting for me. A donkey moves along the road when it is rapped with a stick and it was the same for us, but my father struck us much harder than he would have struck a donkey.

The mention of a donkey brings to mind another memory of my mother. I took the flocks to graze as usual, then came back to the house quickly to clean the stable. My mother was with me and she hurried me because we had to go out to pick figs too. We loaded the crates on to the donkey's back, because the figs grew a long way beyond the village. I can't place this story in time, except that this particular morning seems now to have been close to the incident of the green tomato. It was the end of the season, because the fig tree I can see us standing before is bare. I tied the donkey to its trunk to prevent it eating the fruit and leaves that were scattered on the ground.

I began to pick and my mother said, 'Pay attention, Souad. You stay here with the donkey, and pick up all the figs on the side of the road but don't go further than this tree. Don't move from here. If you see your father arrive with the white horse, or your brother, or somebody else, whistle and I'll come quick.' She moved off down the road to join a man on a horse who was waiting for her. I knew him by sight: his name was Fadel. He had a round head, and was small and strong. His horse was well cared-for, very white with a black spot, the tail plaited to the end. I didn't know if he was married.

My mother was cheating on my father with him. I knew it as soon as she told me to whistle if anyone came. The man on the horse disappeared from view, my mother, too. I picked the figs at the edge of the road. There weren't many but I wasn't allowed to look any further away because if I did I wouldn't see my father or anyone else who might come along.

I don't remember feeling afraid that day, perhaps because my mother had laid her plan so well. I took ten steps in one direction, ten in the other, and picked up all of the figs I could find. I had a good view of the road looking towards the village: I could have seen anyone approaching from a distance and have plenty of time to whistle. I couldn't see Fadel or my mother, but I guessed they were about fifty paces away, hidden somewhere in the field. If someone were to arrive suddenly she could always pretend that she went off for a moment on urgent personal business. A man, even my father or brother, would never ask an indecent question about such a thing: it would be shameful.

I wasn't alone for long. The crate was still half empty when I saw my mother come out of the field, then Fadel getting back on to his horse.

He missed the saddle the first time because the horse was tall. He had a pretty wooden riding-whip, finely made, and he smiled at my mother before he rode away. I pretended to have seen nothing. The whole thing happened quickly. They had made love somewhere in the field, sheltered by the grass, or they just talked together. I didn't want to know. My mother did not confide in me. And she knew that I wouldn't say anything because I was an accomplice. If I did I'd be beaten to death, too. My father only knew how to beat women and make them work. So if my mother had made love with another man on the pretext of gathering figs, it didn't bother me. She had good reason.

Then we had to gather the figs very quickly so that the crates would be full enough to justify the time we'd been away from the house. Otherwise my father would ask: 'You bring back empty crates. What were you doing all that time?' And I'd get the belt.

Eventually my mother got on to the donkey, her legs straddling its neck, close to its head so that she did not crush the figs. I walked in front to guide the animal along the road.

Soon we encountered an elderly woman, alone with a donkey, who was also gathering figs. Since she was elderly, she could be out alone. As we caught up with her, my mother greeted her and we continued on our way together. This road was narrow and difficult, full of holes, bumps and stones. In places it rose steeply and the donkey had trouble advancing with his load. At one point he stopped dead at the top of a slope before a big snake and refused to go on. My mother hit him and encouraged him but he tried to move back, trembling with fear, like me. I hate snakes. Fortunately, the old woman seemed not at all afraid of the snake, despite its size. Suddenly I saw it roll up, twist, and slither into the ditch. She must have struck it with her walking-stick. The donkey agreed to move on.

There were a lot of snakes around the village, small ones and big ones. They would even nest in the house, in the storeroom between the sacks of rice, or in the piles of hay in the stable.

We saw them every day and were as frightened of them as we were of grenades. Since the war with the Jews, grenades had been everywhere. You didn't know if you would die when you put your foot down. I heard them talk about it at home, when my father's father visited, or my uncle. My mother warned us about the grenades, which were almost invisible among the pebbles and larger stones, and I watched the ground constantly as I walked along. I don't remember having seen one but the danger was always there.

When we got home my father wasn't there, which was a relief because we were late. It was already ten o'clock. At that hour in the morning the sun is high, and we had to get the figs out of the heat before they shrivelled and softened. They had to be in good condition, carefully prepared, for my father to sell them at the market. I liked packing the crates of figs. I would choose beautiful fig leaves, big green ones, to carpet the bottom of the crates. Then I would place the figs in neat rows, like beautiful jewels, and put more large leaves on top to protect them from the sun. It was the same for the grapes: we cut them off the vine with scissors and cleaned them carefully, removing any damaged ones or dirty leaves. I lined those crates with vine leaves and covered the grapes as I did the figs so that they would keep fresh.

My father also sold the cheeses I had to make. I would pour the *halib*, milk, into a large metal bucket, then skim off the yellow fat that formed at the edges, and the cream, which I set aside for making *laban*, which was sold in separate packets for Ramadan. The *laban* were put into large buckets for my father, who made up the packets with heavy plastic so that the product wouldn't spoil. It was my job to attach the label.

I made yogurt and more cheese with the skimmed milk. When I had formed them, I turned them into a piece of muslin, tied a knot, and squeezed so that the liquid ran out. Then I put them on to a big platter and covered them with a cloth so that the sun and the flies wouldn't damage them. Later I would wrap them in white packets. My father went to the market almost every day during the fruit and vegetable season, and twice a week with the cheeses and yogurt.

My father did not get behind the wheel of the van until it was loaded, and woe betide us if we hadn't finished in time. My mother sat beside him and I was wedged between the crates in the back. It was a good half-hour's ride and when we arrived I could see big buildings. It was the city, a pretty, clean city. There were lights to control the traffic, and I remember a shop window with a mannequin in a bride's dress. I twisted my head to catch glimpses of the shops for as long as I could; I wasn't allowed to walk about and certainly could not go into them.

I would have loved to wander round the city, but when I saw girls walking on the pavement wearing short dresses, with their legs bare, I was shocked. If I had encountered them close up I would have spat on their path. They were *charmuta*, I thought. They were walking all alone, without parents next to them. They would never be married. No man would ask for them because they had shown their legs, and they were made up with lipstick. I didn't understand why they weren't locked in. Were those girls beaten as I was? Were they slaves like me? Did they work as I did? I wasn't allowed to move an inch from my father's van. He supervised the unloading of the crates, collected the money, then signed to me that I must climb in and hide inside. For me the only pleasures of the trip were being free of work, and the glimpses of the boutiques through the crates of fruits and vegetables. Now I understand that life in my village hadn't changed since my mother was born, and her mother before her, and for many previous generations of women.

The market was large with a roof that was covered with vines and provided shade for the fruit. When everything had been sold, my father was happy. He always counted the money several times, then put it into a small cloth sack that was tied with a string and hung round his neck.

When my sister went to the market with my parents, I would clean the courtyard, then make things to eat. I sat on the ground, put flour on a large flat plate with water, salt and yeast and worked it into dough with my hand. Then I left it to rest under a white cloth, and rise. Meanwhile I stoked the bread oven to get it really hot. The bakehouse had a wooden roof, and inside the iron oven was always burning. The live coals stayed hot but the fire had to be stoked before we cooked on it, especially before making bread. I made a big pancake, a beautiful round loaf, and a flat one that always had to be shaped in the same way. If it wasn't, my father would throw it in my face. After the bread was baked, I would clean the oven and pick up the cinders. When that was finished, my hair, my face, my eyebrows and eyelashes were grey with dust.

One day, I was in the house and saw smoke coming from the roof of the bakehouse. I ran with my sister to see what was happening and we heard someone shout, 'Fire!' My father came with water. There were flames and everything was burning. Inside the bakehouse there were what looked like blackened goat droppings. I had forgotten a loaf inside the oven and had not cleaned out the cinders so a fire had started. I shouldn't have forgotten the bread or to take out the live embers.

As I expected, my father beat me harder than he ever had before. He kicked me, beat my back with a cane, caught me by the hair, pushed me to my knees and forced my face into the cinders, which were, fortunately, only warm. I almost suffocated because the ash went into my nose and mouth. I was weeping when he released me, all black and grey with red eyes. It was a very serious crime, and if my sister and mother hadn't been there, I believe my father would have thrown me into the fire.

The oven had to be rebuilt with bricks and the work took a long time. Every day I slunk to the stable bent low and swept the courtyard with my head down. I think my father loathed me. But apart from this one mistake, I had always worked well. I did all of the family laundry in the afternoon before night fell, beat the sheepskins, swept, cooked, fed the animals, cleaned out the stable. Moments of rest were rare: when we weren't working for ourselves, we helped other villagers and they did the same for us.

We girls were never out at night. But my father and mother often went to the neighbours, or to visit friends. My brother went out too, but not us: we didn't have any friends and my older sister never came to see us. The only person outside the family whom I saw sometimes was a neighbour, Enam. She had a spot in her eye and people made fun of her; everyone knew she had never been married.

From the terrace I could see the villa of the rich people. Sometimes I heard them laugh. They ate outside, even late at night, but in our house we were locked up like rabbits in our rooms. In the village, I remember only this rich family, not far from our house, and Enam, the old maid, who was always alone, sitting in front of her house.

There were several girls of more or less the same age as we were in the village and, in season, we were all taken by bus to pick cauliflowers in a big field. I remember so well this huge field of cauliflowers. It was so big you couldn't see the end of it and we felt we would never finish. The driver was so small that he sat on a cushion to be able to see over the steering-wheel. He had a small round head with close-cropped hair.

All day long we cut cauliflowers on all fours, all the girls in a row, supervised by an older woman with a stick. We piled the cauliflowers up in a big truck. At the end of the day, the truck stayed in the field and we got back into the bus to return to the village. There were many orange trees on either side of the road, and because we were thirsty the driver stopped and told us to go and pick an orange each, then come back. 'One orange and *halas!*' he said, which meant 'One but not two!'

Soon we were all running back to the bus and the driver, who had parked on a little side-road, reversed towards us. Suddenly he turned off the engine, got out and started to yell. He had run over a girl. A wheel of the bus had rolled over her head. As I was in front, I bent down and tried to raise her head by her hair. But it was stuck to the ground. I passed out.

The next thing I remember, I was in the bus on the knees of the woman who was supervising us. The driver was stopping before every house to let the girls off. When I got out in front of our house the supervisor explained to my mother that I was sick. She put me to bed and gave me a drink. She was good to me that night because the woman had explained to her what had happened. She had to explain the accident to each mother while the driver waited. I wondered if he wanted to be sure that everyone was told the same thing.

It was odd that it happened to that particular girl. When we were gathering cauliflowers, she was always in the middle row, never at the edges. Among us, when a girl is always protected by others it means she might run away. And I had noticed that she was always surrounded, that she wasn't able to switch places in the line and no one spoke to her. It was forbidden even to look at her because she was *charmuta*. If anyone did speak to her, they, too, were treated as *charmuta*. Had the driver deliberately run over her?

The police came to question us and took us in the bus back to where it had happened.

There were three officers, and that was really something for us to see – men in uniform. We could not look them in the eye, and had to be very respectful. We showed them the exact spot. I bent down. There was a dummy head on the ground and I raised it with my hand as I had the girl's. They said to me: '*Halas, halas, halas* . . .' And that was it.

We got back into the bus to find that the driver was weeping. He drove fast and wildly. The bus bounced on the road and I remember that the supervisor held her chest with both hands because her breasts were bouncing, too. The driver went to prison: it had not been an accident.

For a long time after this I was sick. I kept seeing myself raising the girl's crushed head and I was afraid of my parents because of everything they were saying about her. They said she was *charmuta*. She must have done something bad, but I didn't know what it was. I couldn't sleep at night, kept seeing the crushed head and hearing the sound of the tyres when the bus reversed. In spite of all the sufferings I have endured, an image of the girl has stayed with me. She was the same age as I, with a short, pretty haircut. It was bizarre that she had short hair: the girls in the village never cut their hair. Why had she? She was different from us, better dressed. What had turned her into a *charmuta*? I never knew. But I knew in my own case.

As I continued to grow up, I waited hopefully for a marriage proposal. But no one asked for Kainat, and she didn't seem concerned – she was resigned to remaining an old maid. I found this awful, for her and for me, because I had to wait until Kainat was married before I could take a husband. I began to feel embarrassed at others' weddings. In terms of freedom, marriage was the most I could hope for, but even married, a woman risked her life with the least lapse in her conduct. I remember a woman who had four children. Her husband must have worked in the city because he always had on a jacket. When I saw him in the distance he was always walking fast, kicking up a storm of dust behind him. His wife's name was Souheila, and one day I heard my mother say that the village was telling stories about her. People thought she was involved with the owner of the shop because she went there so frequently to buy bread, vegetables and fruit. Maybe she didn't have a big garden like ours, or maybe she was seeing this man secretly – as my mother had seen Fadel. One day my mother said that her brothers had gone into her house, cut off her head and walked around the village with it. Mother also said that when her husband returned from his job he was happy to learn that his wife was dead because she'd been suspected of having an affair . . . but she wasn't very pretty and she already had four children.

I didn't see those men walk through the village with their sister's head, I only heard the story from my mother. I understood what had happened but I wasn't afraid, perhaps because I hadn't seen it for myself. It seemed to me that in my family nobody was *charmuta*, that these things couldn't happen to me. The woman had been punished for breaking the rules, and that was normal. It was certainly more normal than

THE BRIDE'S BLOOD

Hussein's parents came to ask for Noura and returned to discuss it several times. In my country, a girl is sold into marriage for gold, so Hussein's parents brought the gold, which they displayed in a pretty gilded dish, and his father said: 'There! Half for Adnan, the father, and the other half for his daughter, Noura.'

If there isn't enough gold, you continue negotiating. The two shares are important because on the day of the wedding the girl is supposed to show everyone how much gold was given to her father in exchange for her. But the gold Noura wore on her wedding day was not really for her: the number of bracelets, the necklace, the diadem she received reflected her parents' honour – and her own. It is shameful for a girl and her family if she has no jewellery on her wedding day. My father forgot that when he yelled at us that we weren't worth as much as a sheep. When he sold a daughter, he was owed half of the gold he demanded as her price.

When the business is concluded, there is no paper to sign: it is the men's word that counts. Only the men's. The women – the mothers and the bride – have no say.

No one else in the family saw the gold when Noura and Hussein were betrothed, but we all knew the marriage had been agreed because Hussein's family had come to us. We had to keep out of sight, and cause no disturbance during the men's negotiations.

Noura knew that a man had come to the house with his parents, so she would be married. She was pleased. She told me she wanted to be able to dress better, pluck her eyebrows, have a family of her own. Noura was anxious while the fathers were in discussion. She wanted to know how much gold the family had brought, and prayed they would come to an agreement. She didn't know what her future husband looked like, or how old he was, and she could not ask. It is shameful to ask such questions.

A few days later, my father summoned Noura in my mother's presence, and told her she would be married on such-and-such a day. I wasn't there to hear this because I didn't have the right to be with them. I shouldn't even say 'I didn't have the right,' because rights do not exist in my country for women. There are customs, that's all. If your father points to a corner of the room and tells you to stay in that corner for the rest of your life, you won't move from there until you die. If your father places an olive in a plate and tells you that today that's all you'll have to eat, you only eat that olive. It is difficult to get out of this role of consenting slave. As a female you're born into it. For all of your childhood, you are taught to be obedient to men – by father, mother, brother, and then by your husband.

When Noura reached this much hoped-for status, she must have been seventeen.

But maybe I'm mistaken. As I reflect on and try to order my memories, I've realized that my life then had none of the personal landmarks that Europeans celebrate. No birthdays, no photographs. It was more like the life of a small animal who eats, works, sleeps and is beaten. You know that you are 'mature' when you're in danger of drawing down the wrath of society at the least false step. And at this 'mature' age, marriage is the next step. Normally, a girl is mature at ten and is married between fourteen and seventeen. Noura was approaching the limit.

The family began to prepare for the marriage, and alerted the neighbours. As the house was not large, they rented the common courtyard for the reception. It was an attractive place, a sort of flower garden where there were grapevines and space for dancing. A covered veranda provided shade and would shelter the bride.

My father selected the sheep for the feast. The youngest lamb is always chosen because the meat is tender and doesn't need much cooking. If it has to cook for a long time people say that the father is not well off because he has served an old sheep and has not fed his guests well. His reputation in the village will suffer, and his daughter's even more. My father went into the stable, grabbed the animal he had selected and dragged it into the garden. He tied its hoofs to keep it still, took a knife and cut its throat. Then he took the head and twisted it a little over a large dish to make the blood flow. I watched this with disgust. The lamb's legs were still moving.

When my father's task was done, the women took over. They boiled water to clean the inside of the carcass, and set aside the intestines. Then the animal was skinned – my mother performed this delicate operation. The skin had to remain intact. With her big knife, she separated the skin from the meat, and pulled it off with a precise movement. This came away gradually until the hide was separate from the carcass. She would dry it, then either sell or keep it. Most of the skins from our sheep were sold. But people don't think much of you if you take a single sheepskin to the market: you need to display several to show that you are rich.

At nightfall on the day before the wedding, my mother worked on my sister. She took an old pan, a lemon, a little olive oil, an egg yolk and some sugar. She dissolved and mixed all of the ingredients in the pan, then closed herself into a room with Noura to remove all of Noura's pubic hair. Absolutely every single hair of the genital area must be removed. It must be bare. My mother told me that if you forget a single hair, the man would leave without even looking at his wife, saying that she is dirty.

Hair on that part of a woman's body is considered dirty in my culture. We don't shave our legs or our underarms, only the vulva. We pluck the eyebrows too, but that is to make ourselves more attractive. When hair begins to appear on a girl it is the first sign, with her breasts, that she is becoming a woman. And she will die with her hair, since we will be taken back just as we have been created. And yet all the girls are proud of having their pubic hair removed: it is the proof that they will belong to a man other than their father. Without hair you become *someone*. It seemed to me then that it was more a punishment than anything else because I could hear my sister yelling. When she came out of that room the little crowd of women, who were waiting behind the door, tapped their palms and made their ululations. There was great joy: my sister was ready for her marriage and the famous sacrifice of her virginity. When they had all seen her and verified that everything had gone according to the rules, the women returned to their houses.

At sunrise the next day, the food was prepared in the courtyard. Everyone had to see this process and count the number of dishes, and you can't afford to spoil the preparation of a single handful of rice or the whole village will be talking about it. Half of the courtyard was given over to the food: meat, couscous, vegetables, rice, chickens, sweets and cakes that my mother made with the neighbours' help — she would never have been able to do all this by herself.

When the dishes had been shown off, my mother went with another woman to prepare my sister. The bridal dress was ankle-length and embroidered in front, with cloth buttons. When Noura was ready she looked magnificent, covered with gold, beautiful as a flower. She wore bracelets, necklaces and — what counts for more than anything on a bride — a diadem. It was made of a ribbon of gold. Her loose hair was rubbed with olive oil to make it shine. She was helped on to her 'throne', a chair covered with a white cloth, which stood on a table, and sat there to be admired by everyone before the arrival of her future husband. All the women jostled each other to get into the court-yard to view her, all the while making their ululations.

The men danced outside, rather than mingling with the women in the courtyard. We girls were not even allowed to be at the window to watch them. Soon Noura would see what her fiancé looked like. My mother might have given her some idea of his appearance, told her some-thing about his family, his job, his age, but perhaps not. Perhaps all they told her was that his parents had brought the right amount of gold.

Finally my mother placed a veil over my sister's head, and moments later Hussein arrived. He approached Noura, who kept her head lowered under the veil and her hands demurely on her knees to demonstrate her good upbringing. This moment is supposed to be the pinnacle of a young woman's life. I watched with the others, and envied her. I had always been envious of her for being the eldest, for being able to go everywhere with our mother while I slogged away in the stable with Kainat. I envied her for being the first to leave the house. Every girl would like to be in the bride's place on her wedding day, in a beautiful white dress, covered with gold; and Noura was so beautiful. I was only disappointed that she was not wearing shoes. I had seen women in the street, going to the market, wearing shoes. Perhaps because the men always wore them, shoes were for me a symbol of freedom. I wanted to walk without pebbles and thorns tearing my feet. Noura was barefoot – but Hussein wore beautiful polished shoes.

Hussein came towards my sister. Another

chair had been placed beside hers, also covered with a white cloth, on the table. He sat on it, raised her veil, and the ululations resonated in the courtyard. The ceremony was over. The man had just discovered the face of the woman who had remained pure for him and would give him sons. They remained seated, like mannequins. All the others danced, sang, ate, but they didn't move. They were brought food and someone covered them with white towels so they didn't soil their beautiful clothes. As is customary, Hussein didn't touch his wife, kiss her or take her hand. Nothing was exchanged between them, no gesture of love or tenderness. They were a fixed image of marriage and sat there for a long time.

I didn't know anything about that man, his age, if he had brothers or sisters, what he worked at, and where he lived with his parents. But he was from the same village. You don't go looking for a woman anywhere but your own village. It was the first time that I, too, had seen him. We hadn't known if he was handsome or ugly, short, tall, fat, blind, awkward, with a twisted mouth, if he had a big nose, or even if he had ears. In fact, Hussein was an attractive man. He was not very tall, had short, curly hair, his face was tanned, and his nose was short and rather flat with broad nostrils. He looked well fed, and walked proudly. At first glance, he didn't look nasty but something told me that he might be.

At a wedding, to make it clear that the celebration is ending and the guests are expected to leave, the women sing to the husband: 'Protect me now. If you don't protect me, you are not a man . . .' and then: 'We are not leaving here until you dance.' To conclude the ceremony, the husband touches his wife with a finger – she belongs to him now – helps her down and they dance together. Some couples don't dance because they are shy. My sister danced well with her husband.

Then the husband takes his wife home to the house his father has given him. Without a house, he is not a man. Hussein's house was in the village, not far from my parents'. The bridal pair went off on foot alone. We cried as we watched them go. Even my brother was in tears. We wept because she had left us, because we didn't know what would happen to her if she was not a virgin for her husband. We were anxious, but we had to wait until her husband displayed the white linen from the balcony or attached it to the window at daybreak so that everyone could verify the presence of the bride's blood. As many people as possible from the village should come to see it – two or three witnesses are not enough. Otherwise the proof might be contested.

I remember their house, their courtyard. There was a stone and cement wall around it. Everyone was standing there, waiting. All of a sudden my brother-in-law came out with the linen, and that set off the ululations. The men whistled, the women sang, clapping their hands, because he had presented the linen. Hussein tacked it up on the balcony with white clothes pegs. The wedding was all in white, the pegs were white. The blood was red.

Hussein acknowledged the crowd with a wave and then went inside.

★ ★ ★

The sheep's blood, the blood of the virgin, always blood. I remember that, on every Eid, my father killed a sheep. The blood filled a basin and he would dip a rag in it, then paint it on the front door and the floor. To come to the house, you had to pass through this door painted with blood. Everything he killed made me sick with fear. When I was a child, I was forced, like other children, to watch my father kill chickens, rabbits, sheep. My sister and I were convinced he could twist our necks like a chicken's, drain our blood like a sheep's. The first time I was so frightened that I hid between my mother's legs, but she made me look. She wanted me to know how my father killed so I would be part of the family, so I wouldn't be afraid. But I was always afraid: the blood represented my father.

The day after the wedding, along with everyone else, I looked at my sister's blood on the white linen. My mother was weeping, and so was I – we cry a lot at this ceremony to show our joy and salute the honour of the father who has kept the bride a virgin. And we cried with

relief because Noura had passed the great test –
the only test of her life, except when she had to
prove that she could produce a son. I was happy
that she'd married, because it would soon be my
turn. At that moment I didn't think of Kainat,
even though she had to be married before me.

When the guests had gone home, we had to
dismantle the courtyard. It's the job of the
bride's family to wash the dishes and clear up, and
there was much to do. Sometimes the neighbour
women come to help, but not always.

After her marriage, Noura didn't come home
often: she had to take care of her family. But a
short time after the wedding, less than a month,
she came back to our house, crying and com-
plaining to our mother. I couldn't ask what had
happened so I spied on them from the top of the
stairs. Noura was showing her bruises. Hussein
had struck her so hard that she had bruises on
her face, too. She lowered her pants to show her
violet thighs and my mother wept. He must
have dragged her on the ground by her hair, all
the men do that, but I didn't find out why he
had beaten her. Sometimes it's enough if the

young bride can't cook very well, forgets the salt, or there's no sauce because she forgot to add a little water. That's reason enough for a beating. It was my mother in whom Noura confided because my father was too violent: he would have sent her back without listening to her. Mother listened to her, then said: 'He's your husband. It's not serious. You're going home.'

And Noura went back. To the husband who had 'corrected' her by beating her with a stick.

She had no choice. Having seen my sister in that state, I might have decided that marriage meant no more than being beaten by a different man. But despite Noura's experience, I still wanted more than anything to be married. It's a curious thing, the destiny of Arab women – in my village, at least. We accept beating as natural. No thought of rebellion occurs to us. We know how to cry, hide, lie if necessary to avoid the stick, but to rebel? Never. This is because there is no other place for us to live than in the house of our father or husband. Living alone is inconceivable.

Hussein didn't come looking for his wife. Anyway, she didn't stay long because my mother was so afraid her daughter wouldn't want to leave. Later, when Noura became pregnant and they were hoping for a boy, she was the princess of her in-laws, her husband and my own family. Sometimes I was jealous: she was more important than I was in the family. Before she was married, she spent more time with my mother, and afterwards they were even closer. When they went together to gather the wheat, they talked a lot. Sometimes they would close themselves into the room that was used for storing wheat, flour and olives. Its door was green. I would pass it, feeling alone and abandoned, because behind it my mother was with my sister. It was in there that my mother had removed Noura's pubic hair.

I don't know why this door came into my memory so suddenly. I went through it almost every day, carrying sacks. Something frightening happened behind it . . . but what? I think I hid between the sacks out of fear. I see myself like a monkey, crouching on my knees in the dark —

this room doesn't have much light – I am hiding there, my forehead pressed against the small brown floor tiles. My father had painted the spaces between them white. I'm afraid of something. Now I can see my mother. She has a sack over her head. My father has put it there. To punish her? To kill her? I can't cry out. My father pulls the sack tight behind her head. I see her profile, her nose, against the cloth. He holds her hair in one hand and grips the sack with the other. He is dressed in black.

Something must have happened a few hours earlier. What was it?

My sister came to the house because her husband was beating her. Mother listened to her. It seems to me that my memories are confused around that green door. My sister's visit, me hiding between the sacks of wheat, my mother being suffocated by my father with an empty sack. I must have gone in there to hide. I hid in the stable, in that room or in the armoire in the hallway where they left the sheepskins to dry before they were sold. I didn't often hide between the sacks in the storeroom,

I was too afraid of snakes. If I was hiding there it was because I feared something bad would happen to me, too.

Perhaps it was the day my father tried to smother me with a sheepskin, in a room on the ground floor. He wanted me to tell him the truth: was my mother cheating on him? He folded the sheepskin in half and pressed it over my face. I would rather have died than betray my mother, even if I'd seen her with a man. Anyway, if I told the truth he'd have killed us both. Even with a knife to my throat, I couldn't have betrayed her. Did he let go of me or did I escape? Either way, I had run to hide downstairs, behind that green door, between the sacks, which looked like monsters. I used to dream that at night my father emptied the wheat out of them, then filled them with snakes.

There! That is how the pieces of my former life try to find their place in my memory. A green door, a sack, a father who wants to suffocate either my mother or me, my fear of the dark and the snakes.

Not long ago, I was emptying a wastebasket

into a large rubbish bag and a piece of plastic got caught. As it fell back into the wastebasket it made a particular sound. I jumped as if it had been a snake. I was trembling and began to cry like a child.

My father knew how to kill a snake. He had a special cane, with two hooks at the end. He would trap the snake between the hooks so it couldn't move, then kill it with a stick. If he was capable of immobilizing snakes to kill them, he could also put one into a sack so that it would bite me when I plunged in my hand to take out some flour. That was why I was so afraid of that green door. And because no one had yet asked for me in marriage. But I had heard a rumour that when I was barely twelve a family had spoken to my parents about me, officially. There was a man for me somewhere in the village. But I would have to wait. Kainat was ahead of me.

ASSAD

I was the only one to run to him when his horse slipped and he fell off. I will always have this picture of my brother in my mind: he was wearing a colourful green shirt, which billowed behind him because it was windy. He was magnificent on his horse.

I think that I loved him even more after Hanan's disappearance. I wasn't afraid of him. I didn't think he would harm me – perhaps because I was older than him, or because we were closer. But he beat me, too, when my father wasn't there. He even attacked my mother once. They were arguing, he pulled her hair and she was crying. I see them clearly now but don't know what they were arguing about. I always have difficulty with reassembling images and working out their significance. It is as if my old memory has been fragmented during the new life I have had to build in Europe.

Today it is difficult to understand why Hanan had to die, and I certainly didn't understand then. Perhaps she had done something wrong – but Assad was maddened with rage that evening, humiliated at being kept away from his wife, demeaned by his in-laws. Had the news of the baby's death been telephoned to him? Had Hanan spoken to him rudely? I don't know. Violence towards women in my family and in our village occurred daily. And I loved Assad so much. The more my father detested his son, the more I adored my only brother.

His wedding was an extraordinary celebration. It is probably the only memory of real joy I have in the madness of my past. I must have been about eighteen, already old. I had refused to go to another wedding because the girls were making fun of me by then, nudges with the elbow, unpleasant laughter when I passed by.

And I cried all the time. Sometimes I was ashamed to go into the village with my flock, afraid of the looks. I wasn't any better than the neighbour with the defective eye whom nobody had wanted. My mother had allowed me to stay away from that wedding as she understood my despair. That was when I dared to speak to my father: 'But it's your fault! Let me get married!'

He hit me about the head. 'Your sister must be married first! Get out!'

I said it once but not twice.

For my brother's wedding, though, the whole family was happy and no one more than I. Her name was Fatma, and I couldn't understand why Assad was marrying into a strange family from another village. Was there no family near us with a marriageable daughter? My father rented buses for us all to go to the wedding, one for the women and one for the men – the men's in front, of course.

We crossed the mountains, and every time we passed a sharp bend the women gave thanks to Allah with ululations for protecting us from the ravine. The countryside resembled a desert, and the road wasn't paved, just dry black earth. The wheels of the men's bus stirred up a huge cloud of dust in front of us. Everyone was dancing. I had a tambourine between my legs and shook it to accompany the women's ululations. I danced, too, with my scarf – I was good at that. Everyone was joyful, and the driver was the only one not dancing.

My brother's wedding was a much bigger celebration than my sister's. His wife was young, beautiful, short and dark. She was almost Assad's age. In our village, they made a little fun of my father and mother because my brother 'had to' marry a girl of mature age, who was not known in the village. He should have married a girl younger than himself. 'It's not normal to marry a girl your own age! And why look for her outside the village?'

My father gave a lot of gold in exchange for her, and she wore many jewels. The wedding lasted three days, with dancing and feasting. Now I can see myself with my scarf and my tambourine. My heart was happy, I was proud of Assad. He was like a god to us. And this is strange: I'm still incapable of hating him, even if he is a murderer. In my eyes he is 'Assad the *ahouia*'. Assad my brother. *Assad ahouia*. Hello, my brother Assad. Today I never go to work without saying to him, 'Good morning, my brother Assad.' True devotion. As children we shared many things. After he was married, and brought his wife to live with us, I continued to serve him. If there was no hot water for his bath, I heated it for him, I cleaned the bath, I washed and put away his underwear. Now it doesn't seem right that I should have served him with so much love because he was like all the other men.

Soon after the wedding, he beat Fatma, who shamed him by returning to her parents' house. Contrary to custom, her father and mother did not force her back to our house the same day. They were perhaps richer, more advanced than us, or as she was their only daughter, perhaps they loved her more, I don't know. I think that the scenes between my father and brother began because of that. My brother had wanted this woman from another village; he had obliged his father to give a great deal of gold for her, and the result was that she had a miscarriage instead of giving him a son, and brought dishonour to us by returning to her family. I wasn't present, of course, at the family meetings, and there is nothing in my memory to justify what I'm saying now, but I remember perfectly my father on the terrace with that basket of stones, throwing them at Assad's head. And the armoire that Assad had wedged against the door of his room to stop my father entering. Perhaps Assad wanted the whole house to himself. He behaved as if it belonged to him. I think my father felt Assad was taking his place and his money. He often told my brother that he was still a child. In my culture, it's a serious humiliation to say that to a man.

Assad rebelled all the more because he was very sure of himself and much too spoiled. He was the prince of the family. He would shout: 'This is my house!' My father wouldn't put up with that. People in the village asked what foolish thing Fatma had done, why she went with a virgin who has been bought for her husband, not of a loving relationship between a man and a woman. Where is love?

But I do remember one woman in our village, the wife of the richest man. The family was known for having a luxurious house. Their children went to the school. They had tiling everywhere, even the path to the outside was tiled. Usually paths were just pebbles or sand, sometimes tarred. They had a man to look after the garden and the courtyard, which was surrounded by a wrought-iron fence that shone like gold. You could see this house from a distance. In our culture, we love everything that shines and shimmers. If a man has a gold tooth, he must be rich! And if you're rich, everyone must see it. The rich family's house was modern and quite new, magnificent from the outside. There were always two or three cars parked in front. I never went inside, of course, but when I passed with my sheep, I dreamed. The owner's name was Youssef. He was a tall gentleman, very tanned and elegant. They were very close, he and his wife – you always saw them together.

and properly dressed, even if he was just wearing the traditional clothes. He always had his prayer beads in his hand and would be counting them with his long fingers. He came sometimes to our house to smoke his pipe with my father. One day my mother left the house to spend the night at her parents' because my father had beaten her so severely. She left us alone with him. In our land, a woman may not take her children with her: whether they are boys or girls, they stay with their father. And the older I got, the more he beat her, and the more frequently she left us. My grandfather brought her back by force. She would leave sometimes for a week, sometimes a day, or for a night. Once she left for at least a month and my grandfather stopped speaking to my father.

I think that if my mother had died, she would not have had a burial like Mr Youssef's wife, and my father would not have wept or torn his shirt. He did not love my mother. I should have been convinced that love didn't exist in our culture – at least, not in our house. As for me, I had only my brother to love, despite his violence and his outbursts of madness. My sisters loved him, too. Noura had left, but Kainat protected him like me.

Apart from the little sisters, who were too young to daydream about marriage, there were only the two of us in the house. Kainat wasn't ugly, just not very pretty. I was small and slender, but she was rather robust, and her breasts were too large. The men liked women to be a little fleshy but they didn't care for such a large bosom. She didn't know how to make herself more attractive, which made her sad. In fact, neither of us could make ourselves prettier than God had made us. We had no beautiful dresses, always the same white or grey trousers, no makeup or jewellery. And we were locked up like chickens, scratching at the dirt, until we set foot out of the house with our sheep, noses down, eyes on our feet.

If Kainat had no hope, which closed the door to marriage for me, at least I knew that a man had asked for me. My mother said to me: 'Faiez's father came. He asked for you for his son. But we can't discuss marriage for the time being, we have to wait for your sister.' Since then I imagined that he was waiting for me, growing impatient at my parents' refusal. Assad knew him. Faiez lived in the house opposite ours, on the other side of the road. They weren't peasants like us, they didn't work much in their garden. His parents had three sons, and Faiez was the only one who wasn't married. There were no girls in the house, which was why it was not surrounded by walls. Instead it had an attractive low fence, and the door was never locked. The walls were pink and the car parked in front was grey.

Faiez worked in the city. I didn't know what he did, but I supposed he was in an office, like my uncle. He was much better dressed than Hussein, Noura's husband. Hussein was always in workmen's clothes, never very clean, and he smelt bad. Faiez was all elegance, with a beautiful car that he drove off in every morning. I began to spy on his car to get a look at him. The best spot for this was the terrace, where I shook out the sheepskin carpets, picked grapes and set out the laundry to dry. I could always find something to do up there. I noticed that he always parked his car in the same place, a few steps from the door. I couldn't stay too long at a time on the terrace, so it was several days before I had established that he left at about seven every morning, when it was easy for me to find something to do out there.

The first time I saw him I was lucky. I cleaned the stable in a hurry, and I brought dry hay for a sick ewe that was about to lamb. I had taken two or three steps with the hay when he came out, as elegant as my uncle, in a suit, with beautiful black and tan laced shoes, carrying a briefcase, very black hair, tanned complexion, a proud bearing.

I lowered my head, my nose in the straw. I heard him walk to the car, the clacking sound of the door closing, the engine starting and the tyres crunching on the gravel. I raised my head only when the car was in the distance, and waited for it to disappear, my heart thudding in my chest and my legs trembling. And I said to myself: 'I want this man for my husband. I love him. I want him, I want him . . .'

But what to do? How could I plead with him to beg my father to conclude the marriage?

How could I even speak to him? A girl does not speak first to a man. She is not even supposed to look directly at him. Even if this man wanted to marry me, it was not for him to decide it. It was my father, always him, and he would kill me if he knew I lingered for a second with my load of hay to draw Faiez's attention.

I didn't hope for much that day but I wanted him to see me, wanted him to know that I was waiting, too. So I decided to do everything I could to meet him in secret and speak to him, at the risk of being beaten or stoned to death. I didn't want to wait any longer for Kainat to leave the house. It might take months or years. I didn't want to grow old with the mockery of the village. I didn't want to lose all hope of going away with a man, of being free from my father's brutality.

Every morning and evening, I vowed, I will be on the terrace watching for my beloved, until he looks up at me and gives me a sign. A smile. If not, he will ask for another girl from the village or somewhere else. And one day I will see another woman getting into that car in my place. She will steal Faiez from me.

was probably April. In my village, we didn't measure time in the same way as we do in Europe. We never knew exactly how old our parents were, or even knew the date of our birth. Time is calculated by Ramadan and by the seasons. The sun is our guide and it marks the beginning and end of the working day.

At the time this all happened, I believed I was about seventeen years old. Later I discovered from a document that I was nineteen, but I don't know where it came from. Perhaps my mother confused the birth of one daughter with another when she had to give me an official existence. I was mature from the time my periods started and eligible for marriage. I would become a woman on my wedding day. My own mother was still young in years but seemed old; my father looked old because he didn't have many teeth left. Faiez was certainly older than I, but that was a good thing. I expected security from him. My brother Assad was married too young, to a girl of his own age. If she didn't give him sons, one day he would take another woman.

One morning I heard Faiez's footsteps on the

gravel. I shook my wool rug over the edge of
the terrace and he looked up. He saw me and I
knew he understood although he made no sign
and not a word was spoken. He got into his car
and drove off. My first rendezvous, an un-
forgettable emotion, lasted as long as it takes to
eat an olive.

The next morning, I was more adventurous.
I pretended to be chasing a goat so that I could
pass in front of his house. Faiez smiled at me,
and because the car didn't start up straight away,
I knew he was watching me go off towards the
fields with the animals. In the morning the air
was cooler, so I could wear my red woollen
jacket, my only new piece of clothing, which
buttoned up to the neck. It made me prettier to
look at. If I could have danced in the middle of
the sheep I would have. My second rendezvous
had lasted longer, because when I turned my
head just a little at the edge of the village, I saw
that he had still not started the engine. I couldn't
go any further in taking the initiative: he had to
decide how to speak to me in secret. He knew
where I went and when.

The next day my mother went to the city with my father, my brother was with his wife, and Kainat was taking care of the stable and our little sisters. I was alone when I went out to cut grass for the rabbits. After I'd walked for a quarter of an hour, Faiez appeared in front of me. He said hello. His sudden presence stunned me. I looked around uneasily to make sure my brother wasn't coming, or someone from the village. There was no one. I went towards the shelter of a high embankment at the edge of the field and Faiez followed me. I looked down at my feet, twisting the fabric of my dress, and pulling at the buttons of my jacket. I didn't know what to say.

He assumed an attractive pose, a stem of green wheat between his teeth, and looked me over. 'Why aren't you married?'

'I have to find the man for me, and my sister has to be married first.'

'Your father has spoken to you?'

'He told me your father came to see him a long time ago.'

'Are you all right at home?'

'He'll beat me if he sees me with you.'

'Would you like us to get married?'

'My sister has to be the first.'

'You're afraid?'

'Yes, I'm afraid. It's dangerous for you, too. My father could beat both of us.'

He sat down calmly behind the embankment, while I moved quickly to gather the grass. He seemed to be waiting for me but he knew very well that I couldn't go back to the village with him. I asked him to stay there a few minutes to give me a chance to return alone. Then I walked quickly back to the house, proud of myself. I wanted him to have a good impression of me and think of me as a good girl. I had to be careful of my reputation as far as he was concerned, because I had made the first move.

I had never been so happy. It was so wonderful to be with him, so close, even for a few minutes. I felt it in my whole body. I couldn't think about it clearly, I was too naïve – I was no more educated than a goat – but that wonderful feeling was about the freedom in my heart, and my body. For the first time in my life I was *someone*, because I had decided to do as I wanted. I was alive. I was not obeying my father or anyone else. On the contrary, I was breaking the rules.

I have a pretty clear memory of those moments and the ones that followed. Before this experience I had had almost no sense of myself. I didn't know what I looked like, whether or not I was pretty. I wasn't aware of being human, of thinking, of having feelings. What I had always known was fear, the suffering and humiliation of being tied up like an animal in the stable and beaten so hard I had no feeling in my back . . . the terror of being suffocated or thrown into the well. I had received so many blows without resisting. Even if my father couldn't run very fast any more, he always found a way to catch hold of me. It was easy for him to bang my head on the edge of the bath because I knocked over some water, to hit me on the legs when the tea arrived late. You can't think about yourself when you live like this. My first real meeting with Faiez, in the field of green wheat, gave me, for the first time in my life, an idea of who I was. A woman, impatient to see Faiez, who loved him and who was determined to become his wife at any price.

The next day, on the same road, he waited for me to go to the field and came to join me.

'Do you look at other boys besides me?'

'No. Never.'

'Do you want me to speak to your father about the marriage?'

I wanted to kiss his feet. I wanted him to go at that very moment, to run and announce to my father that he, Faiez, didn't want to wait, that he must ask my family for me, bring gold for me and jewels, and prepare a great feast.

'I'll give you a sign for the next time, and don't wear your red jacket. It's too visible and that's dangerous.'

The days passed, the sun rose and set. Morning and evening I watched from the terrace for a sign from him. I was certain he was in love with me.

The next time we were to meet, he didn't come. I waited a long time, more than a quarter of an hour, risked being late getting home and having my father come after me. I was anxious and unhappy, but the time after that he was there. From a distance, I saw him coming down the road. He signalled for me to hide at the end of the field, behind the embankment where no one could see us because the grass was so high.

'Why didn't you come?'

'I did come, but I hid further off to see if you might be meeting someone else.'

'I don't see anyone.'

'The boys whistle when you pass.'

'I don't look at anyone. I'm a good girl.'

'Now I know that. I've seen your father. We'll be married soon.'

He had gone to see my father after the second meeting. And even if the date wasn't fixed, the year wouldn't end without my being married. It was warm and beautiful that day, the figs were not yet ripe but I was sure I wouldn't have to wait for the beginning of summer and the harvests before my mother got the hot wax ready to prepare me for my wedding night.

Faiez came closer to me, very close. I closed my eyes, I was a little afraid. I felt his hand behind my neck and he kissed my mouth. Immediately I pushed him away without speaking, but my gesture said: 'Look out. Don't go any further.'

'See you tomorrow. Wait for me, but not on the road, it's too dangerous. Hide here, in the ditch. I'll meet you after work.'

He was the first to leave. I waited for him to be far enough away before I went home as usual, but more nervously this time. His kiss, the first of my life, overwhelmed me. And the next day, as I watched him approach my hiding-place, my heart was trembling. No one in the house suspected my secret meetings.

In the mornings, my sister sometimes went with me to take the sheep and the goats to pasture but she usually returned home to take care of the stable and the house, and I remained alone in the afternoons. The grass was tall in spring and the animals took advantage of it. It was thanks to them that I could be away by myself. It was a false freedom that my family granted me, because my father watched the time of my departure and return. The village, the neighbours, they were all there to remind me of the consequences of misbehaviour. I communicated with Faiez by almost invisible signals from the terrace. From a movement of the head I knew he would come. But if he got into his car without looking up, he wouldn't. That day I knew he would come – he confirmed it for me. And I felt strongly that something would happen.

I was afraid Faiez wanted more than a kiss, and I wanted it too, without knowing what was waiting for me. I was afraid that if he went too far and I pushed him away, he would be angry. I also had confidence in him because he knew that I couldn't let myself be touched before marriage. He knew very well that I wasn't a *charmuta*. And he had promised me marriage. But I was afraid all the same, all alone in the field with the flock. Hidden in the tall grass, I watched the animals and the road. I didn't see anyone. The field was magnificent with all the flowers, and the sheep were calm. They spent the springtime eating, not wandering off as they did in the height of summer when the grass was scarce.

I was expecting him to come up on my right side, so I was surprised when he arrived from the other direction. That was good: he was cautious about not being seen, he was protecting me. He was so handsome. He was wearing trousers that were tight from the waist to the knee and wide from the knee down, the fashion for men who dress in the modern Western way. He had a white sweater with long sleeves, a V-neck, which exposed the hair on his chest. I thought him elegant next to me. I had obeyed him: I hadn't worn my red jacket. My dress was grey, and also my trousers. I had washed my clothes carefully because, with the work, they were often dirty. I'd concealed my hair beneath a white scarf, but I missed my beautiful jacket. I would have liked so much to be prettier.

We sat on the ground and he kissed me. He placed his hand on my thigh. I pushed it off. He looked annoyed. 'Why don't you want to? Come on!'

I was so afraid that he'd go away, that he'd look for somebody else. He could do that whenever he wanted: he was a good-looking man, my future husband. I loved him, but I didn't want to give in – I was too afraid. But I was even more afraid of losing him: he was my only hope. So I let him do what he wanted without knowing what was going to happen to me, and how far he'd go. He was there, before my eyes, he wanted to touch me, nothing else mattered.

The sun would be setting soon, and I had to take the sheep back. He pushed me into the grass, and did what he wanted. I said nothing, I didn't resist. He wasn't violent, didn't force me, but the pain took me by surprise. I wasn't expecting it, but that was not why I cried. He said nothing, either before or after, he didn't ask me why I was crying, and I wouldn't have known what to say to him if he had. I was a virgin, I knew nothing about love between a man and a woman, no one had taught me anything about it. The woman was supposed to bleed, with her husband, that was all I'd learnt since my childhood. He did what he wanted in silence, until I bled, and all of a sudden he looked surprised, as if he hadn't expected that.

Did he think I had already done this with other men? Because I was alone with my sheep? But he had said he had watched me and had seen I was an honest girl. I didn't dare look at him, I was ashamed.

He raised my chin and said: 'I love you.'

'I love you, too.'

I didn't understand then that he was proud of himself. It was only much later that I felt angry that he had doubted my honour, that he had used me when he knew how much I was risking. I didn't want to make love with him hidden in a ditch, I wanted what all the girls of my village wanted: to have the ritual hair removal, to have a beautiful dress, to be married and to go to bed in his house. I wanted him to show everyone at sunrise the white linen with the red stain. I wanted to hear the women's ululations. He had taken advantage of my fear: he had known I would give in to keep him.

I ran to hide nearby, to wipe the blood off my legs and straighten my clothes while he calmly put himself in order. Afterwards, I begged him not to drop me, to arrange the marriage quickly.

I was a girl who was no longer a virgin and that was serious.

'I'll never drop you.'

'I love you.'

'I love you, too. Now, go back, change your clothes and act like nothing happened. Especially don't cry in the house.'

He left ahead of me. I'd stopped crying but I felt a little sick. The blood was disgusting. Making love with a man wasn't a celebration. I felt bad, I felt dirty, I had no water to wash myself, nothing but the grass to wipe myself with. I still felt the burning in my belly, and I had to collect the sheep, and return home, with my dirty pants. I'd have to wash them in secret, I thought. As I hurried back, I thought I probably wouldn't bleed again but wondered if I would always feel so bad with my husband. Would it always be so disgusting?

Was my expression normal when I reached the house? I wasn't crying any more but I hurt inside and I was afraid. I knew what I had done. I wasn't a virgin any more. I was not safe because I was not married. I wouldn't be a virgin on my wedding night. But that's not important because he knows I was a virgin with him, I reminded myself. I'll arrange it somehow, I'll cut myself with a knife, I'll stain the marriage linen with my blood. I will be like all the other women.

I waited for three days. I watched from the terrace for Faiez to give me a signal for a meeting. This time, he led me into a little shelter of stones, at the other end of the field. It was where my sister and I sat to be out of the rain. That time I didn't bleed. I still had discomfort but less fear. All I cared about was that he would come back. He was there and I loved him even more. What he did with my body wasn't important, it was in my head that I loved him. He was my whole life, all my hope of leaving my parents' house, of being a woman who walked with a man in the street, who got into a car with him to do the shopping and went out to buy dresses and shoes. I was happy to be with him, to belong to him. He was a man, a real one, a capable man. I was confident about the marriage. He didn't know when, and neither did I, but I didn't ask any questions. In my mind, it was certain.

Until it happened, I had to take care that no one denounced me. For the next meeting, I'd change my route. I worked out the extra time I'd need, and in the meantime I didn't dare leave the house alone by the iron door. I waited to be with my mother or sister. I watched for Faiez to leave every morning. As soon as I heard his steps on the gravel, I went quickly to the cement wall. If someone else was outside I turned my back; if there was no one I waited for the signal. Two more rendezvous since the one when I lost my virginity. We couldn't see each other every day, it wouldn't have been wise. It was another six days before he gave the signal for the next meeting. I was still afraid, and still confident. I paid attention to the slightest noise in the countryside. I avoided waiting at the side of the road and instead sat in the grass in a ditch, with my stick. I watched the bees in the wild flowers, and dreamed about the day soon to come when I wouldn't be guarding sheep and goats any more, when I wouldn't be cleaning out the manure in the stable. He was going to come, he loved me, and when he left again I would say to him: 'Don't abandon me.'

We made love for the third time. The sun was yellow. I had to milk the sheep and the cows. I said: 'I love you, don't abandon me. When will you come back?'

'We can't see each other right away. We'll wait a little. We have to be careful.'

'For how long?'

'Until I give you a sign.'

My love affair had gone on for two weeks, three meetings in the field with the sheep. Faiez was right to be careful, and I had to be patient, I knew, wait for my parents to speak to me, as they had spoken to my sister Noura. My father couldn't still be waiting to marry Kainat before me! Since Faiez had asked for me and she was still unmarried at twenty, he could get me off his hands. After all, he had two more daughters! Khadija and Salima, the little ones, would be put to work with my mother, would take over the flocks and the harvesting. Fatma, my brother's wife, was pregnant again, would give birth soon.

She could work, too. I awaited my destiny. Always with a little fear. The days passed and Faiez gave me no sign. I was hopeful all the same, every evening, of seeing him appear out of nowhere, as he did, to the left or right of the ravine where I hid.

One morning in the stable I suddenly felt very strange. The smell of the manure made me dizzy. And later as I prepared the meal, the mutton made me feel ill. I was nervous, I wanted to go to sleep or cry for no reason. Every time Faiez came out of his house he looked somewhere else, made no sign to me. It had been a long time, too long, and I couldn't remember when I last had my period, or when it should arrive. I often heard my mother ask my sister Noura: 'You have your periods?'

'Yes, Mama.'

And, too: 'You haven't had your period? That's good, it means you're pregnant!'

I checked myself several times a day. Every time I went to the bathroom, I looked to see if there was any blood. Sometimes I felt so strange that I thought it must have come. But there was still no blood. And I was so afraid that the fear gripped my throat as if I was going to vomit. I didn't feel as I usually did, I didn't want to work, to get up. My nature had changed. I tried to find a reason that wasn't the worst one. I asked myself if the shock of not being a virgin any more could change a girl this way, could stop her periods. Of course I couldn't ask anyone. The least question on this subject would bring thunderbolts down on me. I thought about it at every moment of the day and especially at night before I fell asleep near my sisters. If I was pregnant my father would smother me in the sheepskin blanket. In the morning when I got up I was happy just to be alive.

I was afraid someone in the family would notice that I wasn't normal. I wanted to vomit at the thought of a plate of sugared rice. I wanted to go to sleep in the stable. I felt tired, my cheeks were pale. Soon my mother would notice and ask if I was ill. So I hid, I pretended to be fine, but it became more and more difficult. And still Faiez didn't appear. He got into his car wearing his beautiful suit, with his briefcase and his fine shoes, and he took off so fast that his car made a cloud of dust.

Summer came. I was supposed to take the animals out at dawn and bring them back before the sun was too strong. I couldn't be on the terrace any more watching for him, although I absolutely had to speak to him about the marriage. Because a strange spot had appeared on my nose. A small brown spot that I tried to hide because I knew what it meant. Noura had the same thing when she was pregnant. My mother looked at me with surprise: 'What have you done to yourself?'

'It's henna. It was on my hands and I rubbed my nose, I wasn't paying attention.'

After that I purposely smudged my nose with henna. But the lie couldn't go on for long. I was pregnant and it was a month since I'd seen Faiez.

I had to speak to him. One evening, when the sun was not yet down, I boiled water in the garden to do the washing so that I could be on the terrace with my laundry at about the time I knew he would come home. This time, I gave him a signal with my head and I kept gesturing to make him understand: 'I want to see you, I'm going down there, you must follow me . . .'

He had seen me and I ran off to wait for him, pretending I had to watch over a sick sheep in the stable. The ewe really was sick, we were waiting for her to lamb, and it wasn't the first time I'd stayed near her. I'd even slept on the straw a whole night for fear of not hearing her.

He arrived at our rendezvous spot a little after me, and he immediately tried to make love, convinced that was why I had called him. I drew back. 'No, that's not why I wanted to see you.'

'Well, why then?'

'I want to talk to you.'

'We'll talk after. Come on!'

'You don't love me. Can't we meet just to talk?'

'Yes, but I love you, I love you so much that every time I see you I want you.'

'Faiez, the first time I wanted nothing, then

you kissed me, and I accepted three times. Now I haven't had my period.'

'Maybe it's just late?'

'No, I've never been late and I feel strange.'

He didn't want to make love any more. His face had gone blank.

'What are we going to do?'

'We have to get married now! We can't wait. You have to go and see my father. Even if there isn't any wedding, I don't care!'

'They'll talk in the village! It's not done! What would we do about putting out the sheet on the balcony?'

'Don't worry about that, I'll take care of it.'

'But we can't have a small ceremony. We said a big wedding – we'll have a big wedding. I'll talk to your father. Wait for me here tomorrow at the same time.'

'But it's not always possible for me. You're a man, you do what you want. Wait for me to give you a sign. If I can, you'll see me braiding my hair. If I don't take off my scarf, don't come.'

The next day, I said I was going to gather some grass for the sick sheep. I gave the signal and ran to the meeting-place, trembling. My father had said nothing, I'd heard nothing. I was so afraid that I couldn't breathe.

Faiez arrived a good half-hour after me. I attacked him: 'Why haven't you gone to see my father?'

'I don't dare look your father in the face. I'm afraid.'

'But you have to hurry, it's been almost two months now. My stomach is going to start getting big. What am I going to do?' And I started to cry.

'Stop it, don't be crying when you go home. I'm going to see your father tomorrow.'

I believed him, I wanted so much to believe him. Because I loved him and I had good reason to hope, because he had already asked my father for me once. I understood that he was afraid to face him. It wasn't easy to explain why he wanted the marriage to take place so soon. What reason could he find, in the face of my father's mistrust, without revealing the secret and destroying my honour and his own before the family?

I prayed to God that night, as usual. My parents were very religious – my mother went often to the mosque. The girls were supposed to say their prayers twice a day in the house. The next day when I woke up I thanked Allah that I was alive.

When I went out on the terrace the car had already left. Then I did my work as usual. I cared for the sheep, cleaned the stable; I brought out the flock, picked the tomatoes. I waited for evening. I was so afraid that I picked up a big stone and struck my stomach with it, hoping to make myself bleed and put things right.

THE LAST MEETING

Evening had come. I was desperate for Faiez to arrive, alone or with his parents, but I knew very well that he wouldn't. It was too late for today. The car wasn't parked in front of his house, and the shutters were closed. I spent the night awake, trying to make myself believe that he had gone to see his family somewhere, that if the shutters were closed it was because of the heat.

It is extraordinary how those few weeks of my life have stayed imprinted on my memory. I, who have so much difficulty reconstructing my childhood, except for the images of cruelty, the absence of happiness and peace, have never forgotten those moments of stolen freedom, of fear and hope. I can see myself so clearly that night under my sheepskin cover, my knees under my chin, holding my stomach with my hands, listening for the least sound in the dark. Tomorrow he'll be there . . . Tomorrow he won't be there . . . He's going to rescue me, he's going to abandon me . . . It was like music playing in my head that wouldn't stop.

The next morning, I saw the car in front of the house. I said to myself: 'He's alive!' There was hope. I couldn't go to watch for him to leave, but in the evening when he returned I was on the terrace. I signalled for a meeting the next day before sunset. And at the end of the afternoon, just before sunset, I went to fetch hay for the sheep. I waited ten minutes, a quarter of an hour, hoping that perhaps he'd hidden a little further off. The harvest was over but in certain places in the field I could collect some good sheaves. I lined them up near the path and knotted them. I worked quickly but I was careful to leave three sheaves untied in case somebody passed by because I was very visible in that spot. If anyone came I'd only have to bend over my sheaves and look very busy at my work, which I'd already finished. That gave me a quarter of an hour extra before I had to go back to the house. I'd told my mother I'd return with the hay in half an hour. At that time of day, the sheep had already been brought in, the goats and the cows, too, and I still had to milk them for the next day's cheeses. I'd employed about every pretext to be at the rendezvous: I had been to the well to draw water for the animals, which required three short trips with a big bucket balanced on my head. The rabbits needed grass, the chickens needed grain that I had gone to collect. I wanted to see if the figs were ripening. I needed a lemon for the cooking, I had to relight the fire in the bread oven.

I was always mistrustful of my parents, who were mistrustful of their daughter. A daughter might get up to many things. Is she going into the courtyard? What is she doing there? She hasn't arranged a tryst behind the bread oven? She's going to the well? Did she take the bucket with her? Haven't the animals already been

more hope of going on living. And I had understood. He had taken advantage of me and had had a fine time. I tore at my hair. It was too late. I'll never see him again, I thought. A week later, I'd even stopped watching for him from the terrace. The shutters of the pink house were closed. He had fled in his car like a coward. I couldn't ask anyone for help.

At three or four months, my stomach began to get larger. I could still conceal it pretty well under my dress but as soon as I carried a bucket or any load on my head, with my back arched and arms raised, I had to make a considerable effort to hide it. And the spot on my nose: I tried to rub it off, but it wouldn't go away. I couldn't try the henna again – my mother wouldn't have believed me.

My anguish was strongest at night. I often slept with the sheep. The pretext was ready-made: when a sheep is about to give birth, it calls out like a human; if help isn't at hand, the little one can suffocate in the mother's womb. I sometimes think about one particular ewe, whose baby was having trouble getting out. I had to put my arm all the way into her, very gently, to turn the lamb's head in a better direction and pull it towards me. I was afraid of hurting it, and I struggled a long time to retrieve this little lamb. The mother wasn't able to push, the poor thing, and I had to give her a lot of help. An hour later she died.

The lamb was a little female. She followed me about like a child. As soon as she saw me leave, she called to me. I milked the ewes first, then fed her with a bottle. I helped many sheep give birth but that is the one I remember. The little one followed me in the garden, she went up the stairs of the house. She was behind me everywhere I went. The mother was dead and the lamb was alive . . .

It's strange to think that we would make such an effort helping a sheep give birth when my mother was suffocating her children. At the time I certainly didn't think about it. It was a custom that you had to accept. When I let these images play in my mind today, I am appalled. If I'd had the awareness that I have today, I would have strangled my mother to save even one of those little girls. But for a woman who was submissive to the degree that my mother was, it was normal to kill girls. For a father like mine, it was normal to chop off his daughter's hair with sheep shears, and to beat her with a belt or a cane or to tie her up in the stable all night with the cows. What would he do to me when he found out that I was pregnant? My sister Kainat and I thought that being tied up in the stable was the worst thing that could happen to us, our hands tied behind our backs, a scarf stuffed into our mouths so we wouldn't yell and our feet bound with the rope he used sometimes to beat us. Mute, awake all night, we just looked at each other, thinking the same thing: 'As long as we're tied up we're still alive.'

And it was my father who came towards me, on a washing day, his cane striking the ground of the courtyard. He stopped behind me. I didn't dare get up. 'I'm sure you're pregnant,' he said.

I dropped the laundry into the basin. I didn't have the strength to look up at him. I couldn't let myself appear surprised or humiliated. And I wouldn't have been able to lie if I'd looked at him. 'No, Father.'

'Oh, yes! Look at yourself! You've got big. And that spot there, you say it's from the sun, then you say it's henna! Your mother has to see your breasts.'

So it was my mother who had suspected. But he was the one to give the order.

'You have to show them.'

Without another word my father went off with his cane. He hadn't struck me. I didn't protest. My mouth was paralysed. I thought, This time I'm dead.

My mother was calm but rough. 'Now, leave the laundry alone! Show me your breasts!'

'No – please, Mother. You're embarrassing me.'

'You show them to me or I'll rip off your dress!'

I undid the buttons from my collar to my chest.

'You're pregnant?'

'No!'

'You've had your period?'

'Yes!'

'The next time you have your period you'll show me!'

I said yes, to calm her down and for my own safety. I knew I'd have to cut myself and smear the blood on a piece of paper to show to her at the next full moon.

I left the washing and went out of the house without permission. I climbed up and hid in the branches of an old lemon tree. It was a silly thing to do, the lemon tree wasn't going to save me, but I was so afraid that I didn't know what I was doing. Very soon my father came to look for me and found me in the branches. He only had to tug on my legs to make me fall. One of my knees was bleeding. He led me back to the house, took some sage leaves, chewed them and applied the pulp to the wound to stop the bleeding. This was strange. I didn't understand why, after making me fall, he would go to the trouble of taking care of me, which he had never done before. I thought, Maybe he believes what I told him. Now, with hindsight, I think it was just to prevent me using this blood to make them think

I'd had my period. After I fell I had a pain in my stomach and hoped my period would come.

A little later, there was a family meeting, which, of course, I wasn't allowed to attend. Noura and Hussein had come. I was listening behind the wall. They were all talking and I heard my father say: 'I'm sure she's pregnant. She doesn't want to tell us. We're waiting for her to show us her period.'

As soon as they stopped talking, I went upstairs and pretended to be sleeping. The next day my parents went to the city. I was forbidden to go out. The courtyard door was closed but I went through the garden and ran to hide in the fields. I started to hit my stomach with a big stone to make the blood come. No one had explained to me how a baby grows in its mother's belly. I knew that at a certain moment the baby moved. I had seen my mother pregnant, I knew how much time it took for the baby to come into the world, but I was ignorant of the rest. From what moment is the baby alive? For me, it was at the moment of birth, since that was when I saw my mother make the choice between letting them live or killing them. What I hoped desperately, although I'd been pregnant for three or four months, was that the blood would come back. That was all I thought about. I couldn't even imagine that the child in my belly was already a human being. And I wept with rage and fear because the stone didn't make the blood come. Because my parents were going to return and I had to get back to the house ahead of them.

This memory is so painful now and I feel so guilty. It's no good telling myself that I was ignorant, terrified of what awaited me. It is a nightmare to think that I hammered like this on my stomach to kill that child.

And the next day, it was the same thing. I hit my stomach with anything I could find, and at every opportunity. My mother had given me a month from the day when she made me show her my breasts. I knew she was counting in her head, and while she waited I wasn't allowed to go out. I had to remain confined to the house and keep to household chores. My mother had said to me: 'You don't go out of that door again!

You're not to watch the sheep, you're not to go out to fetch the hay.' In fact, I could have escaped through the courtyard and the gardens, but to go where? I had never taken the bus alone – anyway, I had no money, and even if I had the driver wouldn't have let me on. I must have been in the fifth month. I'd felt movement in my belly. Like a crazy person, I pressed my stomach against the wall. But I couldn't get away with lying any more or trying to conceal my stomach and my breasts. There was no way out.

The only idea that occurred to me, the only possible one, was to flee from the house and ask my mother's sister to take me in. She lived in the village, I knew her house. One morning, while my parents were out at the market, I crossed the garden, passed the well, jumped over the embankment and made my way to her house. I didn't have much hope because she wasn't very nice, jealous of my mother for reasons I didn't know about. But maybe she'd keep me and find a solution. When she saw me arrive alone, she expressed concern about my parents. Why hadn't they come with me?

'You have to help me, Aunt.'

And I told her everything, about the hoped-for marriage that hadn't happened, about the wheatfield.

'Who is it?'

'His name is Faiez, but he's not here any more. He promised—'

'All right. I'm going to help you.'

She dressed, put on her scarf and took me by the hand.

'Come, we're going to take a walk together.'

'But where? What are you going to do?'

'Come, give me your hand, you can't be seen walking alone.'

I supposed she was going to take me to another woman, a neighbour who had secrets for making a girl's period start or keeping the child from continuing to grow in my belly. Or she was going to hide me somewhere until I was freed.

But she took me home. She pulled me like a donkey that didn't want to move.

'Why are you taking me home? Help me, I beg you!'

'Because that's your place. It's for them to take care of you, not me.'

'I beg you, stay with me! You know what's going to happen to me!'

'This is where you belong! You understand? And don't go out again!'

She forced me to go through the door, turned and left. I saw the scorn in her expression. She must have thought, My sister has a serpent in her house. This girl has dishonoured her family.

My parents had come home. My father closed the door and my mother glowered at me. She made a gesture with her chin and hand that means *charmuta*, slut. 'You dared to go to my sister!' They despised each other: a misfortune happened to one and the other was gleeful.

'Yes, I went to her. I thought she could help me, hide me . . .'

'Go upstairs!'

My whole body was trembling, my legs wouldn't support me. I didn't know what would happen to me once I was locked up in that room. I couldn't make myself move.

'Souad! Get up there!'

After that my sister Kainat stopped speaking to me. She was as ashamed as I was, and she didn't leave the house any more. My mother worked as usual, my other sisters took care of the animals, and they left me locked up like someone with a contagious disease. I heard them talking together now and then. They were afraid that someone in the village might have seen me, that people had started talking. In trying to save myself by going to my aunt, I had especially shamed my mother. The neighbours would know, the tongues would be wagging, the ears would be listening.

From that day on, I couldn't put my nose outside. My father had installed a new lock on the door of the room where I slept and it made a sound like gunshot every night when he secured it. The garden door made the same sound. Sometimes when I was doing the washing in the courtyard, I felt suffocated when I looked at that door. I'll never leave here, I thought. And I believed that, even though I had gone out more than once through the garden and over the embankment when the door was locked. But the prison was secure for any girl in my situation: it would have been worse outside. Outside there was shame, scorn, stones thrown, neighbours who would have spat in my face, or dragged me home by my hair. I didn't even dream about the outside. And the weeks passed. No one questioned me, no one wanted to know who had done this to me, how and why. Even if I accused Faiez, my father wouldn't go looking for him to make him marry me. It was my fault, not his. In my country, a man who has taken a girl's virginity is not guilty, she was willing. And, even worse, she asked for it, provoked the man because she was a whore without honour. I had no defence. My naïveté, my love for him, his promise of marriage, even his first request to my father, nothing counts for anything. In our culture, a man who has self-respect doesn't marry the girl he has deflowered.

Did he love me? No. And if I was at fault, it was in believing that I would hold on to him by doing what he wanted. Was I in love? Was I afraid he would find somebody else? That is not a defence, and even for me it had stopped making sense.

One evening, another family meeting: my parents, Noura and Hussein. My brother wasn't there because his wife was about to give birth and he had gone to be with her and her family. I listened behind the wall, terrified.

My mother spoke to Hussein: 'We can't ask our son. He won't be able to do it – he's too young.'

'I can take care of her.'

Then my father: 'If you're going to do it, it must be done right. What do you have in mind?'

'Don't worry about it. I'll find a way.'

My mother again: 'You'll have to take care of her, but you'll have to do it quickly.'

I heard my sister crying, saying she didn't want to hear this and that she wanted to go home. Hussein told her to wait, then added for my parents: 'You'll go out. Leave the house, you can't be there. When you come back, it will be done.'

I had heard my death sentence with my own ears. I slipped back up the stairs because my sister was about to leave. A little later my father made the tour of the house and the door of the girls' room clanged shut. I didn't sleep. I couldn't comprehend what I had heard. I wondered if it could have been a dream, a nightmare. Were they really going to do it? And if they did, when would it be? How? By cutting off my head? Maybe they would let me have the child then kill me afterwards? Would they keep the baby if it was a boy? Would my mother suffocate it if it was a girl? Would they kill me first?

The next day, I acted as though I'd heard nothing. I was on my guard, but I didn't really believe that they would do it. And then I started trembling again, and I believed it. The only questions were: when, and where? It couldn't happen immediately because Hussein had left. And I couldn't imagine Hussein wanting to kill me.

That same day my mother said to me in her usual tone: 'It's time for you to do the washing.

Your father and I are going to the city.'

I knew what would happen. They were leaving the house just as they'd told Hussein.

Now, when I remember the death of my sister Hanan, I realize that it happened in the same way. My parents were out, we girls were alone in the house with our brother. The only difference in my case was that Hussein had not arrived. I looked at the courtyard: it was a big space, part of it was tiled, the rest covered with sand. It was encircled by a wall, and all around on top of the wall were iron spikes. And in one corner, the metallic grey door, smooth on the courtyard side, without a lock or key, and only a handle on the outside.

My sister Kainat never did the laundry with me — it didn't take two of us. I didn't know what work they'd told her to do, or where she was with the little ones because, of course, she'd stopped speaking to me. She had slept with her back to me ever since I'd tried to escape to my aunt.

My mother was waiting for me to gather up

the laundry. There was a lot of it because I usually did it only once a week. If I began around two or three o'clock in the afternoon, I finished at six in the evening.

First I went for water from the well, at the back of the garden. I arranged the wood for the fire, placed the big laundry tub on it and half filled it. I sat on a stone while I waited for the water to heat. My parents left by the main door of the house, which they always locked on their way out.

I was on the other side, in the courtyard. I had to keep the coals going: the fire was not allowed to burn down because the water had to be very hot before the laundry went in. I had to rub out the stains with olive-oil soap, and eventually go back to the well for the rinse water. It was long and tiring work that I'd been doing for years, but it was even more so now.

I was sitting on a rock, barefoot, in a grey dress, tired of being afraid. I didn't even know any more how long I'd been pregnant with this fear in my belly. More than six months, probably. From time to time I looked over at the door in the back of the courtyard. It fascinated me. If he came, he could only enter by that door.

THE FIRE

Suddenly I heard the door clang. He was there, he was coming towards me.

Twenty-five years later I see these images again as if time has stopped. They are the last images of my life in my village in the West Bank. They play out in slow motion, like films on television. They come back before my eyes constantly. I'd like to erase them as soon as the first one appears but I can't stop the film playing. When the door clangs, it's too late to stop it. Anyway, I need to see it all again, because I'm always trying to understand what I did not understand then. How did he do it? Could I have got away from him if I had understood?

He came towards me, my brother-in-law Hussein in his work clothes, old trousers and a T-shirt. He stood in front of me and said, with a smile: 'Hi. How goes it?' He's chewing a blade of grass. 'I'm going to take care of you.'

That smile, and he said he was going to take care of me. I hadn't been expecting that. I smiled a little too, to thank him, not daring to speak.

'You've got a big belly, huh?'

I lowered my head, ashamed to look at him. My forehead was on my knees.

'You've got a spot. Did you put some henna there on purpose?'

'No, I put the henna on my hair. I didn't do it on purpose.'

'You did it on purpose to hide it.'

I looked at the laundry I was holding in my trembling hands – that's the last fixed and lucid image I have: the laundry and my trembling hands. The last words I heard from him were: 'You did it on purpose to hide it.'

He didn't say any more, and I kept my head down in shame, a little relieved that he didn't ask me other questions.

Suddenly I felt a cold liquid running over my head and instantly I was on fire. Now it was like a movie that has been speeded up, images racing. I started to run in the garden. I slapped at my hair. I screamed. My dress billowed out behind me. Was it on fire, too?

I smelt the petrol and I ran, the hem of my dress getting in the way. My terror led me instinctively away from the courtyard. I ran towards the garden as the only way out. I know I was running and I was on fire and screaming. But I remember almost nothing after that. How did I get away? Did he run after me? Was he waiting for me to fall so he could watch me go up in flames?

I must have climbed on to the garden wall and into the neighbour's garden or the street. There were women, it seems to me, two of them, so I must have been in the street, and they beat at me, I suppose with their scarves. They dragged me to the village fountain and the water hit me suddenly and I screamed in fear. I heard them shouting but I saw no more. My head was down on my chest. I felt the cold water running on me and I cried out with pain because it burnt me too. I was curled up, I could smell grilled meat, smoke. There were a few other vague images, sounds, as if I was in my father's van. But it wasn't his van. I heard women wailing over me. 'The poor thing . . . The poor thing . . .' They were trying to comfort me. I was lying in a car. I felt the jolts of the road. I heard myself moan.

And then nothing, and then again the noise of the car and the women's voices. I was burning as if I was still on fire. I couldn't raise my head, I couldn't move my body or my arms. I am on fire, I thought, still on fire. I stank of petrol. I didn't understand the sound of the car engine, the women's lamentations. I didn't know where they were taking me. If I opened my eyes a little, I could see only a piece of my dress or my skin. It was dark and smelt. I'm still burning but the fire is out, I thought. But I'm burning all the same. In my mind I was still running with fire all over me.

I'm going to die, I thought. That's good. Maybe I'm already dead. It's over, finally.

DYING

I was on a hospital bed, curled up in a ball under a sheet. A nurse had come to tear off my dress. She pulled roughly on the fabric and the pain jolted me. I could see almost nothing – my chin was stuck to my chest and I couldn't raise it, or move my arms. The pain was in my head, my shoulders, my back, my chest. I felt sick. This nurse was so unkind that I was frightened whenever I saw her come in. She didn't speak to me. She tore pieces off me, put on a compress and went away. If she could make me die, she would do it, I thought. I'm a dirty girl. If I was burned it's because I deserved it since I'm not married and I'm pregnant. I knew very well what she was thinking.

Blackness. Coma. How much time passed, days or nights? No one came to touch me, they didn't look after me, they gave me nothing to eat or drink, they were waiting for me to die. And I would like to die, I thought. I am so ashamed of being still alive. I'm suffering so much. I can't move. I would like some oil on my skin to calm the burning, I would like them to raise the sheet so the air might cool me a little.

A doctor came. I saw trouser legs and a white shirt. He spoke but I didn't understand him. The unkind woman came and went. I could move my legs now and I used them to raise the sheet from time to time. I was in pain whether I lay on my back or on my side. I slept, my head still stuck to my chest, as it was when the fire was on me. My arms were extended out from my body and both were paralysed. My hands were still there, but I couldn't use them. I wanted to scratch myself, to rip off my skin to stop the pain.

They made me get up. I walked with the

nurse. My eyes hurt. I saw my legs, my hands hanging on either side of me, the tiled floor. I hated that woman. She brought me into a room and took a shower spray to wash me. She said I smelt so bad it made her want to vomit. I stank, I wept. I was like rotting refuse on which you'd throw a bucket of water. Die. The water tore off my skin. I screamed, I wept, I begged. The blood ran down my fingers. She made me remain standing. Under the stream of cold water she pulled off pieces of blackened skin, the shreds of my burned dress, stinking filth. It formed a little pile on the floor of the shower. I smelt so strongly of rotting burned flesh and smoke that the nurse put on a mask. From time to time she left the room, coughing and cursing me. I disgusted her, I ought to have died like a dog, but far away from her. Why doesn't she just finish me off? I wondered. I returned to my bed, burning and icy, and she threw the sheet over me so she didn't have to look at me. Die, her expression said to me. Die, and let them throw you somewhere else.

My father was there with his cane. He was

furious. He rapped on the ground, wanting to know who made me pregnant, who brought me here, how it happened. His eyes were red. The old man was crying, but he still frightened me with that cane and I couldn't answer him. I would sleep, or die, or wake up. My father was there. He wasn't there any more. But I hadn't been dreaming – even now his voice is still ringing in my head: 'Speak!'

My head was supported by a pillow and I succeeded in sitting up a little. Nothing gave me any relief but at least I could see who passed by in the corridor, since the door was half open. I heard someone, I saw two bare feet, a long black dress, a small form like mine, thin, almost skinny. It wasn't the nurse. It was my mother.

Her two plaits were smoothed with olive oil, her black scarf, that strange forehead, a bulge between her eyebrows over the nose, a profile like a bird of prey. She frightened me. She sat on a stool with her black market bag and started to weep, to snuffle, wiping her tears with a handkerchief, her head rocking back and forth. She wept with shame, for herself and the whole family. And I saw the hatred in her eyes.

She questioned me, her bag clutched against her. I knew the bag: she always carried it with her when she went to the market or to the fields. She carried bread in it, a plastic bottle of water, sometimes milk. I was afraid, but less so than I was in my father's presence. My father could kill me, but not her.

'Look at me, my daughter,' she said. 'I could never bring you home like that, you can't live in the house any more. Have you seen yourself?'

'I haven't been able to look.'

'You are burned. The shame is on the whole family. I can't bring you back. Tell me how you got pregnant. Who with?'

'Faiez. I don't know his father's name.'

'Faiez, the neighbour?'

She began to cry again, jabbing at her eyes with the handkerchief, as if she wanted to force it into her head.

'Where did you do it? Where?'

'In the field.'

She bit her lip and cried even more. 'Listen to me, my child, I hope for you to die. It's better if you die. Your brother is young. If you don't die, he'll have problems.'

Assad is going to have problems? I thought. What sort of problems? I don't understand.

'The police came to see the family at the house. The whole family, your father and your brother, and your mother, and your brother-in-law, the whole family. If you don't die, your brother will have trouble with the police.'

Perhaps she took the glass out of her bag, because there was no table near the bed. No, I didn't see her look in the bag, she took it from the windowsill: it was a glass from the hospital. I didn't see what she filled it with.

'If you don't drink this, your brother is going to have problems. The police came to the house.'

Did she fill it while I was weeping with shame, with pain, with fear? I was crying about a lot of things, my head down and my eyes closed.

'Drink this. It's me who gives it to you.'

Never will I forget that big glass, filled to the top with a transparent liquid, like water.

'You drink this and your brother won't have any problems. It's better for you, it's better for me, it's better for your brother.'

And she was crying, and so was I. I remember that the tears ran down over the burns on my chin, along my neck, and they stung my skin. I couldn't raise my arms. She put her hands under my head and she raised me to the glass she was holding. Until then no one had given me anything to drink. She was bringing this big glass to my mouth. I would have liked at least to dip my lips into it, I was so thirsty. I tried to raise my chin, but I couldn't. Suddenly the doctor came into the room, and my mother jumped. He grabbed the glass from her hand and banged it down on the windowsill. 'No!' he shouted. I saw the liquid run down the glass and spill over the windowsill, transparent, as clear as water. The doctor took my mother by the arm and made her leave the room. I was still looking at that glass, and I would have drunk it, I would have lapped up the liquid like a dog. I was thirsty, as much as for water as for dying.

The doctor came back and said to me:

'You're lucky I came in when I did. Your father, and now your mother! No one from your family will be allowed in here.'

'My brother Assad, I'd like to see him, he is good.'

I don't know what he answered. I felt so strange, my head was spinning. My mother had talked about the police, about my brother who supposedly had enemies. Why him, since it was Hussein who had set fire to me? That glass, it was to make me die. There was still a wet spot on the windowsill. My mother wanted me to drink it and die, and so did I. But I was lucky, according to the doctor, because I had been about to drink this invisible poison. I felt I had been delivered, as if death had tried to charm me and the doctor had made it disappear. My mother was an excellent mother, the best of mothers, she was doing her duty in giving me death. It was better for me, I thought. I shouldn't have been saved from the fire, brought here to suffer, and now take such a long time to die to deliver me from my shame and my family's.

Three or four days later my brother came. I will never forget the transparent plastic bag he brought. I could see oranges and a banana. I hadn't eaten or drunk anything since I'd arrived there. I wasn't able to, and no one had tried to help me. Even the doctor didn't dare. I knew they were letting me die because it was forbidden to intervene in a case like mine. I was guilty in everyone's eyes. I would endure the fate of all women who sully the honour of men. They had only washed me because I stank. They kept me there because it was a hospital where I was supposed to die without creating more problems for my parents and the village. Hussein had botched the job: he had let me run away in flames.

Assad didn't ask any questions. He was afraid and he was in a hurry to get back to the village. 'I'm going to go through the fields so no one sees me. If our parents find out that I've come here to see you there will be trouble.'

I had wanted him to come but I was uneasy having him lean over me. I saw in his eyes that I disgusted him with my burns. No one, not even he, was interested in how much I was suffering in this cracking, decaying, oozing skin, slowly devouring me like a serpent's venom over my whole upper body, my hairless head, my shoulders, my back, my arms, my breasts. I cried a lot. Was it because I knew it was the last time I would see him? Did I cry because I wanted so much to see his children? Later I learnt that his wife had had two boys. The whole family must have admired and congratulated her.

I couldn't eat the fruit. It was impossible alone, and then the bag disappeared. I never saw any of my family again. My last vision of my parents is of my mother with the glass of poison, my father furiously striking the floor with his cane. And my brother with his bag of fruit.

In the depths of my suffering, I was still trying to understand why I hadn't seen anything when the fire reached my head. There had been a petrol can next to me, but there was a cork in it. I didn't see Hussein pick it up. My head was down when he said he was going to 'take care of me' and for a few seconds I'd thought I was saved because of his smile and the blade of grass he was chewing. In reality, he had wanted to gain my confidence to stop me running away. He had planned everything the day before with my parents. But where had the fire come from? The coals? I didn't see anything. Did he use a match? I always had a box next to me, but I didn't see that either. It must have been a lighter in his pocket. Just enough time to feel the cold liquid on my hair, and I was already in flames. I would so much like to know why I didn't see anything.

One night, I lay flat on my back in total darkness. I could see curtains around me; the window had disappeared. I felt a strange pain like a knife stuck into my stomach. My legs trembled. I'm dying, I thought. I tried to sit up but I couldn't. My arms were still stiff, two filthy wounds that were of no use. There was no one, I was alone. So who had stuck this knife into my stomach?

I could feel something strange between my legs. I bent one, then the other. I tried to disengage the thing. I didn't realize, at first, that I was giving birth. I felt around in the darkness with my feet. Without really knowing what it was, I pushed the child's body slowly back under the sheet. I remained still for a moment, exhausted by the effort.

When I brought my legs together, I could feel the baby against my skin on both legs. It moved a little. I held my breath. How did it get out so quickly? A knife stab in the belly and it was there? I'm going back to sleep, I thought. It's impossible. This child didn't come out all alone without warning. I must be having a nightmare.

But I wasn't dreaming, because it was there, between my knees, against my skin. They weren't burned so I had sensation in my legs and feet. I raised a leg, as you would a hand, to brush a tiny head, arms that moved feebly. I must have cried out. I don't remember. The doctor came into the room, parted the curtains, but I was still in darkness. It must have been night time. I could see only a light in the hall through the open door. The doctor leant over and took the baby away, without showing it to me. There was nothing between my legs now. Someone pulled the curtains closed. I don't remember any more – I must have fainted. I slept a long time, I don't know. The next day and the following days, I was certain of only one thing: the child was no longer in my belly.

I didn't know if it was dead or alive, a boy or a girl, no one spoke to me about it, and I didn't dare ask the unkind nurse what they had done with it. I was incapable of giving it a reality. I knew that I had given birth but I hadn't seen the child, it wasn't put into my arms. I was not a mother then, but human debris condemned to death. My strongest emotion was shame.

Later the doctor told me that I had given birth at seven months to a tiny boy, but that he was alive and being cared for. I heard vaguely what he was saying to me, but my ears had been burned and hurt so terribly. I was in pain all over the upper part of my body, and I kept passing from a coma to a half-awake state, with no awareness of day or night. They were all hoping for me to die and they expected it to happen. But I found that God would not let me die so quickly. The nights and days were confused in the same nightmare and in my rare moments of lucidity I had only one obsession: to rip with my nails at my infected stinking skin. But my arms wouldn't obey me.

Someone came into the room once, in the middle of this nightmare. I sensed a presence rather than actually seeing them. A hand passed like a shadow over my face without touching it. A woman's voice, with a peculiar accent, said to me in Arabic: 'I'm going to help you, do you understand?' I said yes, without believing it. I was so uncomfortable in that bed, the object of everyone's scorn; I didn't understand how anyone could help me, especially how anyone could have the power to help. Take me back to my family? They didn't want me. A woman burned for honour is supposed to burn to death. The only way to help me stop suffering was to help me die.

But I said yes to that woman. I didn't know who she was.

Part II
Jacqueline

FINDING SOUAD

My name is Jacqueline. At the time of these events, I was in the Middle East working with a humanitarian organization, Terre des Hommes, which was directed by an extraordinary man, whose name was Edmond Kaiser. I toured the hospitals looking for children who had been abandoned, who were handicapped or suffering from malnutrition. This work is done in collaboration with the International Red Cross, and other organizations involved with Israelis and people from the West Bank. I have a great deal of contact with both populations because I live and work within their communities.

It was only after I had been in the Middle East for seven years that I heard that girls were being murdered by their families because they had had contact with a boy, perhaps only talked to him, often without proof that anything at all had happened. Very occasionally a girl has had an 'adventure' with a boy, which is unthinkable in this culture, given that the father makes all decisions about marriage. Until I heard about Souad, though, I had never been involved in such a case.

To a Western mind, the idea that parents or a brother can murder their own daughter or sister simply because she has fallen in love is in-comprehensible, especially in the twenty-first century. In our society, women are free: they vote, they may have children out of wedlock, they choose their husbands.

But having lived in the Middle East for seven years, when someone spoke to me about such killings, I knew immediately that it must be true, although I had had no personal involve-ment with such a case. It is a taboo subject, which especially does not concern foreigners, and the woman who eventually drew it to my attention knew me as a trusted friend. She is a Christian with whom I am frequently in contact because she works with children. She sees many mothers from villages all over Israel and the West Bank. She is a little like the neighbourhood *moukhtar* – that is, she invites the local women to have coffee or tea and talks with them about what is going on in their village. It is an important custom and form of communication, and it alerted my friend to children in serious difficulty. One day she heard a group of women say that in one of the villages a girl had behaved badly and her parents had tried to burn her to death. They thought she was in a hospital somewhere.

My friend has a certain charisma and she is well respected. She displays enormous courage, which I was about to witness. Normally she is involved only with children, but the mother is never far away. In September of that year, she said to me: 'Listen, Jacqueline, there is a girl in the hospital who is dying. The social-service worker confirmed to me that she was burned by someone in her family. Do you think you can do anything?'

When I asked her what more she knew about the case, she said only that it was a young girl who was pregnant, the village people said she was rightly punished and now she was expected to die in hospital. When I expressed horror, she told me that that was the way things were. The girl was pregnant so she had to die. That was all there was to it. It was quite normal. Everyone felt so sorry for the parents, but not for the girl.

The story sounded an alarm in my head, but children were my first responsibility. However, I said to myself: 'Jacqueline, you must see for yourself what this is about.'

I left for the hospital. It was not one that I was familiar with, but I knew the country and its customs, and I could speak the language. When I arrived I asked to be taken to a girl who had been burned and staff led me to her. I entered a large room where I saw two beds, each occupied by a girl. I sensed that it was an isolated unit, a place where they put the cases they didn't want to be seen. It was a rather dark room, with bars on the windows, two beds and nothing else. As there were two girls, I told the nurse I was looking for the one who had just had a baby. She pointed, 'It's that one!' then left the room. She hadn't even asked me who I was.

One of the girls had short frizzy hair, it looked almost shaved. The other one had medium length straight hair. Both faces were blackened, sooty. Their bodies were covered with sheets. I knew they had been here about two weeks. It was obvious that they were unable to speak. They both looked close to death. The one with the straight hair was in a coma. The other, the one who had had the child, opened her eyes from time to time.

No one came into the room, neither nurse nor doctor. I didn't dare to speak, much less touch them, and the odour that hung in the air was foul. I had come to see one girl, and I had discovered two, both hideously burned, both uncared-for. I went out to look for a nurse in another ward, and when I found one, I asked to see the hospital's medical director.

I am familiar with hospitals. The medical

director received me politely and seemed somewhat sympathetic. I told him about the burned girls and that I worked with a humanitarian organization that might help them.

'Listen,' he said, 'one fell into a fire, and the other – it's the family's business. I advise you not to get involved.'

I told him that my work was giving aid, and especially to people who had no other source of help, and asked if he could tell me a little more.

'No, no, no. Be careful. Don't get involved in this kind of business!'

I knew I couldn't force him to tell me anything so I left it at that, but I went back to the room where the girls were and sat down. I waited, hoping that the girl who had opened her eyes was able to communicate. The other's condition was disturbing. When a nurse walked by in the hallway, I asked about what had happened to the girl who had hair but didn't move.

'Oh, she fell into a fire and is in very bad shape. She's going to die.'

There was no pity in her voice. It was just a

statement of fact. But I did not accept the explanation.

The other stirred. I moved closer to her and stayed there for a few minutes without speaking. I watched her and tried to understand her situation. I listened to the sounds in the corridor. Perhaps someone else would come in, someone I could talk to. But the nurses passed without stopping. To all appearances, the girls were receiving no nursing at all. No one approached me, no one asked me anything even though I was a foreigner dressed in Western-style clothes – always well covered out of respect for local custom and because it is the only way to get anything accomplished. I thought someone might at least have asked me what I was doing there, but they ignored me.

After a little while, I leant over the girl who seemed able to hear me. I didn't know where to touch her. The sheet prevented me from seeing where her body had been burned, but her chin was stuck to her chest, and not much was left of her ears. When I passed a hand before her eyes, she didn't react. I couldn't see her arms or her hands, and I didn't dare lift the sheet. But I had to touch her somewhere to make her aware of my presence. As with a dying person, it was important to make her understand that someone was there, a presence, a human contact. Her legs were bent, with her knees up under the sheet. I placed my hand gently on one knee and she opened her eyes.

'What is your name?' She didn't answer.

'Listen to me. I'm going to help you. I will come back and I will help you.'

'*Aiwa*,' she said. It means 'yes' in Arabic. She closed her eyes. I didn't know if she'd seen me.

That was my first visit to Souad. I left feeling overwhelmed. I was going to do something, I knew that much. In everything I have ever done, I have always felt somehow that I have heard a call. If I hear about someone in distress, I go to them knowing that I must answer that call, I don't know how, but I'll find a way.

I went back to my friend, who was able to tell me more about the girl's case. The child she had given birth to had already been taken away by the social services by order of the police. The girl was young, she went on, and no one in the hospital would help me. 'Jacqueline, believe me, you are not going to be able to do anything.'

The next day when I returned to the hospital, the girl was still only semi-conscious, and her neighbour in the next bed was still in a coma. The fetid odour was unbearable. I was aware of the extent of her burns but I did not need to be told that no one had disinfected them. The following day, one of the two beds was empty. The girl who had been in a coma had died during the night. I looked at the empty bed. It is always painful not to have been able to help, and now I was determined to look after the other. But she was only semi-conscious, and I couldn't understand any of what she tried to tell me.

And this was when what I call the miracle happened, in the person of a young doctor from the West Bank. The medical director had already told me to forget about the girl because she was dying. When I asked this young doctor for his opinion and why they hadn't at least cleaned her face, he said, 'They try to clean her as well as they can but it is very difficult. This sort of case is very complicated because of customs ... you understand.'

'Do you think she can be saved, that something can be done?'

'Since she isn't dead yet, there may be a chance. But tread carefully.'

In the following days, Souad's face was cleaner, and I saw streaks of mercurochrome. The young doctor must have given instructions to the nurse, who had made some effort, at least. Later Souad told me that they had held her by the hair to rinse her in a bath, because no one wanted to touch her. I was careful not to criticize – that would only worsen my relationship with the hospital. I went back to the young doctor, and told him about my work with the humanitarian organization, my interest in trying to help. I asked him again if he thought she had any hope of surviving.

'My opinion is that, yes, she does, something could be attempted, but I don't think that it can be done in our hospital.'

'Well, could we take her to a different one?'

'Theoretically, yes, but she has a family, parents. She is a minor and we can't intervene. The parents know she's here, they have already come, but they have been forbidden to visit again.'

'Listen, Doctor, I'd like to do something. I don't know what the legal obstacles are, but if you tell me she has a chance to live, even the smallest chance, I must try to do something.'

The young doctor seemed a little amazed by my persistence. He certainly must have thought that I didn't understand the situation. I was one of those 'humanitarians' who knew nothing about his country. He was about thirty, tall, thin, dark, and spoke English well. He didn't resemble his colleagues, most of whom will not respond to enquiries from Westerners.

'If I can help you, I will,' he said.

Success! Over the next few days, he talked to me about the patient's condition. Since he had been educated in England, our conversations flowed easily. I learnt that, in effect, Souad had until now received no care. The doctor reminded me that she was a minor, that it was forbidden to move her without her parents' permission. 'And for them she's as good as dead. That's all they're waiting for.'

I asked if he thought they might allow me to take her to another hospital where she would be cared for and better treated. He said that they would not. I went back to my friend, shared with her my idea of having Souad moved and asked if she thought it was possible.

'If the parents want her to die, you won't be able to do anything. It's a question of honour for them in the village.'

In this type of situation if I am dissatisfied with a negative answer, I will press until I find an opening, even a tiny one. And I always pursue an idea to the limit.

'Do you think I can go to the village?'

'You're risking a lot if you do. Listen to me. You don't know how relentless this code of honour is. They want her to die because if she doesn't their honour has not been washed clean and the family is rejected by the village. They would have to leave in disgrace. Do you understand? You can throw yourself into the lion's jaws, but you're taking a big chance for prob-ably no result. She is condemned. Without any care for such a long time, with burns like these, the poor girl won't live long anyway.'

But the next time I went to see Souad, she opened her eyes, listened to me and answered me despite her suffering. When I asked her where her baby was, she said she did not know, that it had been taken away.

'Souad, you must answer me because I want to do something. If we are able to get you out of here, if I can take you somewhere else, will you come with me?'

'Yes, yes, yes. I'll come with you. Where will we go?'

'To another country where all this will be behind you.'

'But my parents . . .'

'We'll see about your parents. You trust me?'

'Yes . . . Thank you.'

I returned to the young doctor and asked if he knew where the village was, where they incinerated young girls for falling in love.

'She comes from a little hamlet about forty

kilometres from here. The road is virtually impassable and it's dangerous because you don't know what goes on there. Often there are no police in remote places.'

'I don't know if I can go there alone.'

'Oh, no! I wouldn't advise you to do that. Even trying to find the place you'll get lost. There aren't any sufficiently detailed maps.'

I may be naïve but I'm not stupid. I knew that it would be hard to persuade someone to tell me how to find the village, and all the more so because it was in territory occupied by the Israelis and I was a foreigner. Also, I, Jacqueline, Terre des Hommes or not, humanitarian or not, Christian or not, might be taken for an Israeli woman come to spy on the people of the West Bank.

I asked if he would come with me.

'That's madness!'

'Doctor, we might save a life. You tell me yourself that there's hope if she's taken some-where else.'

The argument made sense to him because he was a doctor. But he was also from the West

Bank – like the nurses. And as far as the nurses were concerned Souad, or any other girl like her, should die. One already had. I did not know if Souad had a real chance of pulling through but in any case she had received no care. I would have liked to tell the doctor that I found it unacceptable to withhold care from a young girl because that is the custom. I didn't though, because I knew that he was caught in the system. He had already shown great courage in talking to me about it: honour crimes are a taboo subject.

But finally I had half convinced him. He was truly a good man and I was touched when he told me hesitantly that he didn't know if he was brave enough. I said we could only try, and if it didn't work, we'd just come back.

'All right, but you'll let me turn round if there's the slightest complication?'

I promised the young doctor, whom I will call Hassan, that I would.

As a young Western woman, in the Middle East to care for children in distress, be they Muslim, Jew or Christian, I didn't appreciate the risk I was running that day when I got into my car, with the young doctor at my side. The roads are not safe, the inhabitants are distrustful, and I was with an Arab doctor, recently graduated from an English university. Our adventure would have been unthinkable if the goal had been less important. He must have thought I was mad.

When we left in the morning, Hassan was green with fear. I would be lying if I said I was at ease, but with the daring of youth, and my conviction of the rightness of my mission, I plunged ahead. Of course, neither of us was armed.

For me it was 'God be with us.' For him, it was '*Inshallah!*'

We left the city, and were soon driving through the countryside of the West Bank, parcels of land belonging to small farmers. They were surrounded by low stone walls, with little lizards and snakes slipping between the stones. The land, a reddish ochre colour, was dotted with fig trees. The road that led out of the city was not tarred but it was passable. It connected the hamlets and villages with the markets. The

Israeli tanks had just about flattened it but there were enough holes to make my little car rattle. The further we got from the city, the more small farms we saw. If they have enough land, the farmers grow wheat, but otherwise they graze flocks – goats or sheep. The girls labour in the fields and attend school infrequently, if at all; those who are lucky enough to go are soon brought back to care for their younger siblings. I knew that Souad was illiterate.

Hassan knew the road but he had never heard of the village we were looking for. From time to time we asked directions but because my car had an Israeli number-plate and we were in occupied territory, the directions we were given were not necessarily reliable.

After a short time, Hassan said to me, 'This is crazy. We're going to be alone in the village. I telephoned the family to warn them that we were coming, but God knows how they'll receive us. The father by himself? The whole family? Or the entire village? They won't understand your involvement.'

'Did you tell them that the girl was going to

die and we're coming to talk to them about it?'

'Exactly. That's what they're not going to understand. They burned her, and the person who did it is probably waiting for us round the next bend. In any case, they'll tell us her dress caught fire, or that she fell head first into the coals! It's complicated in these families. It would be much better to turn back.'

I tried to boost his courage. I would probably have gone without him, if I'd had to, but in these areas women don't go about alone and I had a better chance of success if he was with me. Eventually we arrived at Souad's village. Her father received us outside, in the shade of an immense tree. I sat on the ground with Hassan on my right. The father sat against the tree with one leg bent, his cane resting on it. He was a small man, with reddish hair and a pale face, freckled, almost albino-looking. The mother remained standing, very erect in her black dress and veil. Her face was uncovered. She was an ageless woman, with strong features, a hard expression. Peasant women often have this look, brought on by their burden of work, children and servitude.

The house was typical of the region, but we didn't see much of it.

Hassan introduced me, then said: 'This woman works for a humanitarian organization.'

And the conversation went on in the time-honoured style between the two men.

'How are your flocks doing? And the harvest? You sell well?'

'The weather's bad. Winter's coming. The Israelis make a lot of problems for us.'

They talked about the weather for some time before they touched on the real subject of our visit. The father did not mention his daughter, so Hassan did not, and neither did I. They offered us tea. Since I was a stranger, I could not refuse the customary hospitality. And then it was time to go.

'We'll come back to pay another visit.'

We were not going to get any further than that, so we left. It was necessary to begin in that way, both Hassan and I knew that. We had to broach the subject slowly and not appear to be enemies, or inquisitors, so that we could return. Then we were back on the road going towards the city. I remember the sigh of relief that escaped me. I felt as if I had been walking on eggs.

'That didn't go too badly, did it? We'll go back in a couple of days.'

'You really want to?'

'Yes. We haven't accomplished anything yet.'

'But what do you hope to offer them? If it's money, don't count on it. Honour is honour.'

'I'm going to play up that she's dying. Unfortunately it's true and you said so yourself.'

'She has scarcely any chance.'

'Well, I'm going to tell them that I will take her somewhere else to die, which would relieve them of the problem.'

'She's a minor and she hasn't any papers. The parents' agreement is needed and they won't give it.'

'We'll go back anyway. You'll phone them again?'

'In a few days. Give me some time.'

Souad didn't have much time. But Hassan

had his job at the hospital and his family to consider. His involvement in an honour crime might bring him serious enemies. I understood and respected his caution. After all, it was he who had to make contact with the village to announce our visits, and that can't have been easy.

SOUAD IS GOING TO DIE

'My brother is kind. He tried to bring me bananas and the doctor told him not to come back.'

'Who did this to you?'

'My brother-in-law, Hussein, my older sister's husband. My mother brought poison in a glass . . .'

By now I knew a little more of Souad's story. She could speak to me more easily, but the conditions in this hospital were terrible. The burns were infected and bled continuously. Her chin was still attached to her chest. She couldn't move her arms. The petrol had been poured over her head, and burned her as it ran down her ears and neck, over her back, arms and chest. She rolled herself into a ball probably when she was being driven to hospital, and she was still in that position more than two weeks later. She had given birth in a semi-coma, and the child had disappeared. The social worker must have left him in an orphanage, but where? I knew only too well the future that awaited an illegitimate child. He had no hope.

My plan was crazy. First I wanted to take her to Bethlehem, which was in Israeli hands at the time, but accessible to both of us. I knew that the hospital there didn't have the facilities to care for a serious burns patient, but this was only a first step. At least they could dispense basic care. In the next phase of the plan Souad and I would leave for Europe, with the agreement of Terre des Hommes, which I had not yet requested. And this did not include the child, whom I had still to find.

When the young doctor got into my car for our second visit to Souad's parents, he was still uneasy. We received the same welcome, outside under the tree, made the same banal conversation until we got up to leave. This time, however, I mentioned their children, whom we never did see. 'You have many children?' I asked. 'Where are they?'

'They're in the fields. We have a married daughter, she has two boys, and a married son, who also has two boys.'

Boys. I had to congratulate the head of the family – extend sympathy too: 'I know that you have a daughter who is the cause of much trouble for you.'

'*Ya haram!* It's terrible what's happened to us! What misery!'

'How sad for you.'

'Yes, it is sad. *Allah karim!* But God is great.'

'In a village, it is painful to have such problems.'

'Yes, very hard for us.'

The mother did not speak. She stood motionless.

'Well,' I said, 'she's going to die soon anyway. She's in very bad shape.'

'Yes. *Allah karim!*'

And the doctor added, very professionally:

'Yes, she is very bad.' He had understood why I had entered into this collusion over the hoped-for death of a young girl, and joined in now with explicit remarks about Souad's inevitable death.

At last the father confided in him the core of their worries: 'I hope we will be able to stay in the village.'

'Yes, of course. In any case, she's going to die.'

'If Allah wills it. It's our fate. We can't do anything about it.'

But he did not say what would happen afterwards. So, I advanced a pawn on the chessboard: 'But it's difficult for you that she will die so close to home. How do you plan to bury her? Where?'

'We'll bury her in the garden.'

'Perhaps, if I took her with me, she could die elsewhere and you wouldn't have that problem.'

Clearly this meant nothing to them, that I would take Souad with me to die somewhere else. They had never heard of such a thing. Hassan understood this and pursued it: 'She is right. All in all, that would mean fewer problems for you, and for the village.'

'Yes, but we will bury her here, if Allah wants it so, and we will say to everyone that we buried her and that will be that.'

'I don't know, just think about it. Perhaps I can take her to die somewhere else. I can do that if it would be good for you.'

It was horrible, but I had to emphasize Souad's death: to speak of medical care and, perhaps, recovery would have horrified them. They told us they needed to talk about it among themselves, which was their way of signalling that it was time for us to leave, which we did after the customary goodbyes, and promises to return.

The doctor and I thought our offer made sense. Souad would disappear, and the family would recover their honour in the village.

'Allah is great, as the father said. We must be patient,' said the doctor.

I continued to go to the hospital every day to try to get Souad at least the minimum of care. My presence obliged the nurses to make a little effort: they disinfected the burns now, but without painkillers and without the specialized products needed for treating severe burns. Poor Souad's skin remained an immense wound, unbearable for her and difficult for others to look at. I thought about the hospitals in Switzerland and France, and other places where they treat burns with such exquisite care to help the skin regenerate with a minimum of scarring and to reduce the pain.

The brave doctor and I returned to negotiations. We stuck with it, setting out the terms as diplomatically as we could.

'It would not be good for her to die in this country. Even there in the hospital that would not be good for you. But she can be taken far away, to another country. And that way it's over, finished, you can tell the whole village that she has died. She will have died in another country and you'll never again hear a word about her.'

The conversation was strained now, but without papers any agreement I reached with the parents was worthless. But I thought I was almost there. I asked nothing else about the situation, neither who caused Souad's injuries nor the identity of the father of her child. Had I brought up these details the family's honour would have been damaged even more. I just had to convince them that their daughter would die, but somewhere else. They must have thought I was mad, but also that I might be of use.

It seemed that the idea was taking root. If they said yes, then as soon as we had turned our backs, they could declare the death of their daughter to the village, without giving any more details, and without the need for a burial in the garden. They could say whatever they liked, even that they had avenged their honour in their own way. It is bizarre from a Western perspective even to imagine such dealings: the bargaining did not disturb them from a moral viewpoint because a special kind of morality is enacted in these areas against girls and women. Legal structures do not protect females: they are based on the interests of the men of the clan. Souad's mother accepted it without flinching.

She wanted her daughter to disappear and die. She could not wish otherwise, and I even found myself feeling sorry for her.

Usually I do not become emotionally involved with the people I work with. In Africa, India, Jordan or the West Bank, I have to adapt to the culture and respect tradition. My goal is simply to help a victim, male or female. But that was the first time I had negotiated for a life in such a fashion.

At last they gave in. The father made me promise, the mother, too, that they would never see Souad again. 'NEVER AGAIN!'

I made the promise but to keep it, I said, I would have to take Souad abroad, and to do that I needed papers for her. 'I'm going to ask you to do something that may seem a little difficult, but I'll be with you and will help you. We have to go together to the office that issues identity and travel documents. I have to take you by car to Jerusalem, you and your wife, for you to sign the papers.'

This new obstacle immediately made them uneasy. Any contact with the Israeli population, and especially with government officials, was hard for them.

'But we don't know how to write.'

'That is not a problem, your fingerprint will be enough.'

They thought about it for a little while. 'All right. We will come with you.'

Before I came back for the parents, I had to prepare the way with the administration officials. Fortunately, I knew people in the Jerusalem visa office, and the clerks knew what I did for children. Indeed, it was a child I was rescuing. Souad had told me she was seventeen, which made her a child. I explained to the Israelis at the visa office that I was going to bring to them the parents of a gravely ill girl from the West Bank and that they could not be kept waiting for three hours or they would leave without signing anything. They were illiterate people who needed me for the formalities. I would bring them, with a birth certificate if they had one, and the officials would have only to confirm the age of the girl on the travel document. I added, pushing my luck once more, that the girl would be leaving with her child. I still didn't know where the baby was or how to find it, but for the moment that was not the issue. First things first: my immediate problem was to get the official approval of the parents and for Souad to receive some treatment.

The Israeli clerk asked if I knew the name of the child's father. I didn't, but I didn't want the child registered as illegitimate on an official document: 'No, don't write that! His mother is going to another country and your statement of illegitimacy won't be well received where she's going.' This document for Souad and the child was not a passport, only a permit to leave the West Bank for another country. She could never return: she would no longer exist in her country, she would have been eliminated, the little burned girl, a phantom. I asked the clerk to make out two documents, one for the mother and one for the infant. The clerk asked the whereabouts of the child and I told him I had to find it.

Time passed, but after an hour the Israeli official gave me the green light, and the next day I was on my way to pick up Souad's parents. I was alone this time. They got into the car in silence, their faces like masks, and we went to the visa office in Jerusalem. For them, this was enemy territory, where they were usually treated as less than nothing. I waited, seated next to them. My presence assured the Israelis that these people had not brought a bomb with them. Suddenly, the employee who authorized the papers signalled to us to come over: 'According to the birth certificate this girl is nineteen. You told me seventeen.'

'We're not going to quibble over this. It's hardly important if she's seventeen or nineteen.'

'Why didn't you bring her with you? She has to sign, too.'

'I didn't bring her because she's in a hospital, dying.'

'And the child?'

'Listen, drop it. You'll give me a travel document for this girl, in front of her parents, and they will sign, and one for the child, too. I'll give you all the details, and then I'll come back for the documents.'

If the security of their territory is not at issue, the Israeli authorities are co-operative. When I started my humanitarian work in the occupied territories, they had given me a hard time. That changed when they came to understand that I also worked with severely handicapped and Down's Syndrome Israeli children, many of whom were the products of family inter-marriage in certain ultra-religious communities. It is the same in some particularly religious Arab families. At that period my work was focused on this problem in the two communities. It had earned me the administration's acceptance.

At last the documents were signed, and we were on our way back to the car. I would take Souad's parents back to their village, the little red-haired man with blue eyes in a white head-cloth, with his cane, and his wife in black, her eyes focused on the hem of her dress.

It was at least an hour's drive between Jerusalem and the village. The first time I had met these people I was very afraid. Now I no longer feared them. I didn't judge them either. I thought only, 'poor people'.

They followed me without a word. They were a little afraid that the Israelis would make trouble for them. I had told them they had nothing to fear, and that everything would turn out all right. Apart from a few essential words, we did not speak. The rest of the family and the inside of the house remained hidden from me. Observing them, it was hard for me to believe that they had wanted to kill their daughter, but even though Souad's brother-in-law had performed the act, it was these people, her parents, who had made the decision that it should be done. The same feelings surfaced in me again later with other parents whom I met in similar circumstances: I could never think of them as murderers. Souad's parents did not cry, but I have seen others who did because they were prisoners of this abominable custom, the honour crime. At their house, they got out of the car in silence, and I left. We would not meet again.

Now there was much to be done. First, I had to get in touch with the head of my agency, Edmond Kaiser, the founder of Terre des Hommes. I had still not spoken to him about my

three or four in the morning and we were going to another hospital. At that time, there were not yet the numerous barricades that were installed at the time of the *intifada* and the trip was uneventful. We arrived in the early morning at the hospital, where everything had been prepared. The medical director knew about the situation and I had asked that Souad should not be questioned about her family, her parents or her village. The hospital received donations from the Order of Malta, was better equipped and much cleaner.

They settled Souad in her room. I planned to visit her every day while I waited to receive the visas for Europe and, especially, for word of the child. Souad didn't talk about him. It seemed that it was enough for her to know that he was alive somewhere. Her apparent indifference was perfectly understandable. After everything that had happened to her, she was psychologically and physically incapable of accepting herself as a mother. As for the baby, he was illegitimate, born of a disgraced mother who had been burned for the sake of family honour.

It was better to separate any such child from his original community. Had it been possible for him to live a proper life in his own country, we would have left him there. For the child, as for the mother, it would have been the least painful solution. But he would have endured the shame of his mother in some orphanage. We owed it to him to get him out. Souad thought only of leaving and asked me about it at every visit. I told her we would leave when we had the visas, and she should not worry. She complained that the nurses tore off her bandages without compunction and yelled every time they came near her. Indeed, the quality of care, although more hygienic, was not ideal, but there was no alternative: we had to wait for the visas.

During that time, I used my contacts to find the baby. The friend who had brought Souad's case to my attention got in touch, a little reluctantly, with a social worker, who reported that she knew where the child, a boy, was but that I could not just take him away. Besides I was wrong, she thought, to want to be encumbered with him: he would be an extra burden for me, and afterwards for the mother. So I discussed it with Souad: 'What is your son's name?'

'His name is Marouan.'

'Was it you who gave him this name?'

'Yes, I did. The doctor asked me.'

Sometimes she was lucid, at others she was suffering from amnesia. She had forgotten the terrible circumstances of the baby's birth, forgotten that they had told her he was a boy, and she had never before mentioned a name to me.

'What do you want to do about him? I don't think we should leave without him.'

She glanced up at me, painfully, because her chin was still attached to her chest. 'You think so?'

'Yes, I do. You're going to get out, but you know how Marouan will have to live if he stays here. It will be hell for him.' He would always be the son of a *charmuta*, a whore. I didn't say this, but she must have known it. Her tone when she said, 'You think so?' was enough for me. It was a positive response.

I began to look for the child. First I visited

one or two orphanages, trying to find a baby of about two months old whose first name was Marouan. But I was not in a strong position to locate him. The social worker despised girls like Souad – she was from a good West Bank family that had not repudiated such traditions. But I knew I'd get nowhere without her. In response to my insistence, and to please my friend, she told me where he had been placed. It was more of a rat-hole than an orphanage, and it would be difficult to get him out. He was a prisoner of the system that had placed him there.

Two weeks later, I had met intermediaries of every stripe. There were those in favour of submitting the child to the same fate as his mother, getting rid of yet another mouth to feed – some such children die without explanation. And then there were those who understood my perseverance. In the end, I had in my arms a two-month-old baby, who had a tiny pear-shaped head, and a little bump on his forehead, a result of his premature birth. He had traces of the classic jaundice of newborns. I had been afraid he would have serious problems: after all, his mother had burned like a torch with him inside her and he had been born in appalling conditions. However, although he was scrawny, which wasn't serious, he was otherwise reasonably healthy, and looked at me calmly with his round eyes.

That night I took Marouan home with me where I had everything I'd need for him. I changed and fed him, then put him into a basket to sleep. I had the visas, the air tickets. Edmond Kaiser would be waiting for us in Lausanne to take us directly to the serious burns section of the university hospital. Tomorrow we would leave.

Souad was carried on a stretcher to the plane for Tel Aviv. She was suffering horribly. When I asked her how she was feeling, she answered simply: 'I am in pain.'

'If I turn you a little, will that be better?'

'Yes, that's better. Thank you.'

Always 'thank you'. Thank you for the wheelchair at the airport – she hadn't seen one before. Thank you for the coffee with a straw. Thank you for settling her somewhere while I got the boarding passes. As I was having trouble balancing the baby while I went through the formalities, I told Souad I was going to place the little one on her so she must not move. She gave me a frightened look. Her burns prevented her taking him properly in her arms. She managed to bring them just close enough together to support him. She made a fearful gesture when I entrusted the baby to her. It was hard for her. 'Stay just like that,' I said. 'I'll be back soon.'

I had been forced to enlist her help: I couldn't push the wheelchair, hold the baby, and handle my passport, the visas, the documents for Souad and the baby, and explain my strange travelling group. Other travellers came up to us to admire the baby, as everyone always does. 'Oh, what a beautiful baby! Isn't he adorable?' They didn't look at the mother, completely disfigured, her head bent over her child. She was bandaged under her hospital gown – it was too difficult to dress her. One of my woollen jackets was draped over her, then a blanket. She couldn't raise her head to thank the passers-by for their kind wishes or to tell me how much this baby, which they found so adorable, panicked her. As I moved away from her to take care of the official business, the surrealistic nature of the scene struck me. She was there, burned, with the baby in her arms. She had experienced hell and so had he, but people passed them with a smile, saying, 'Oh, what a beautiful baby!'

When it was time to board, another problem presented itself: how to get Souad on to the plane. The Israelis brought a huge crane and Souad was wheeled into a sort of cabin suspended from it, then winched up until the cabin was level with the plane door. Two men were there to receive her.

I had reserved three seats for her so that she could stretch out and the flight attendants had arranged a curtain to shield her from the eyes of other passengers. Marouan was in a cradle the airline had provided. We were on a direct flight. Souad didn't complain although the painkilling medication had had little effect. I tried to help her change position from time to time, but nothing helped. She looked a little haggard, but confident. I couldn't persuade her to eat but she would drink through a straw. I looked after the baby, but she avoided looking at him.

She didn't know where Switzerland was, she had never seen an aeroplane before, or a crane, or so many different people in the hubbub of an international airport. She had seen nothing of the world and was suddenly barraged with all sorts of new experiences, which were perhaps terrifying for her. And her suffering was far from over. I did not even know if surgeons would be able to operate on her, whether skin grafts were still possible. Afterwards she would have to integrate into the Western world and learn a new language. When you 'bring out' a victim, as Edmond Kaiser says, you know that you have a responsibility to them for life.

Souad's head was next to the window. 'You see those?' I said. 'They're called clouds.' She was not capable, in her condition, of contemplating everything that awaited her. She hoped, without knowing what for. She slept. Some passengers complained about the smell, despite the curtain drawn around her. Two months had passed since the day of my first visit to Souad, in that dreadful hospital room. The skin on her chest and arms was one vast purulent wound. The passengers could hold their noses and make disgusted faces to the flight attendants, but I was taking a burned woman and her child to their salvation. One day everyone would know why. They would know, too, that there are others, already dead or dying, in every country where the law of men condones honour crimes – in the West Bank, in Jordan, Turkey, Iran, Iraq, Yemen, India, Pakistan and even in Israel. Yes, even in Europe. They would discover that the rare ones who escape must spend the rest of their lives in hiding because their assassins may still be looking for them.

Most of the humanitarian organizations do not take up the cases of these women, because they are 'cultural' cases. And because, in some countries, laws protect the murderers. These women do not attract the big campaigns that are waged against famine and war, to aid refugees or battle against epidemics. My experience demon-strates the difficulty of rescuing the victims of

Part III
Souad

SWITZERLAND

As the infant lay in the plane's cradle, I could gaze at his beautiful little face, long and dark, under the white hospital bonnet. I lost my sense of time and had the impression that it had been only three weeks since he was born, when actually he was already two months old. Jacqueline told me that we arrived in Geneva on 20 December.

I was so afraid when she first handed him to me. I couldn't hold him, and I was in such a state of confusion, shame and pain that I didn't know quite what was happening. I slept most of the time and don't even remember getting off the plane and into the ambulance that took me to the hospital. It was only gradually that I began to understand where I was. Of the extraordinary day when I was taken out of my country I have retained only the memory of Marouan's face and seeing the clouds from the plane window. I knew that we were going to Switzerland, but the word meant nothing to me. I confused Swiss and Jewish because, to me, everything outside my village was an enemy country.

I had no idea about foreign countries and their names. I didn't even know much about my own country outside my village. I was taught that there was my territory and then the rest of the world, the enemy, where 'They eat pork!' as my father used to say. That was how evil he thought they were.

But now I was going to live in an enemy country, with confidence, because 'the lady' was with me. The people around me in the Swiss hospital did not know my story. Jacqueline and Edmond Kaiser had said nothing to them about it. I was a burns victim, and that was the only thing that mattered. The day after we arrived I had an emergency operation, to free my chin from my chest and allow me to raise my head. My flesh was raw and I had lost a lot of weight: I was now only thirty kilos of burns, bones and not much skin. Every time I saw the nurse coming with her instrument table, I started crying because the procedures, which I knew were necessary, were excruciatingly painful. I was given tranquillizers, and the nurse was very gentle – she cut away the dead skin, gave me antibiotics, soothed the pain with creams. There were no forced showers, with gauze ripped off as I had endured in the hospital in my country. At first, my arms hung stiffly at my sides, like a doll's, but eventually the medical staff straightened them so that I could move them. I began to stand, then to walk in the corridors and to use my hands.

At the same time, I was learning about this new world whose language I didn't speak. Since I didn't know how to read or write even in Arabic, I took refuge in silence until I got to know some basic words.

I could only talk to Jacqueline and Hoda,

whom I had met in the hospital, who spoke Arabic. Edmond Kaiser was marvellous: I admired him as I had never admired any man in my previous life. He behaved like a *real* father, I now know, one who had made a decision about my life and allowed Jacqueline to bring me here.

What surprised me when I came out of my room to visit Marouan in the nursery was the girls' freedom. Two nurses went with me: they were wearing makeup, their hair was nicely styled, they wore short dresses, and they talked to men. I thought: 'They're speaking with men, they're going to die!' I was so shocked that I said so to Jacqueline, and later to Edmond Kaiser when I knew the right words.

'Look at that girl over there, she's having a conversation with a man! They're going to kill her.' I sliced my hand across my neck.

'No. Switzerland is not the same as your country. Nobody will harm them. This is normal behaviour in the Western world.'

'But, look, their legs are showing. It's not right to see a girl's legs.'

'Yes, it's quite normal here.'

'And the eyes! It's not a bad thing for women to wear makeup?'

'No, the women here use makeup, they go out, they may have male friends. It's very different from your village. You're in Switzerland now.'

This was not easy for me to grasp or get used to. I must have worn out Edmond Kaiser asking him the same questions over and over again. The first time, I commented: 'That girl, I won't see her again because she's going to die.' But the next day I saw that she was still there and I was happy for her. I said to myself: 'Thank God she's alive. She's wearing the same white blouse, her legs are showing, so it must be all right, and you aren't punished for it.' I had thought that everywhere it was the same as it was in my village. There, if a girl is seen speaking with a man, she is punished severely. I was shocked, too, by the way Swiss girls walked. They were smiling, at ease, and walked with confidence, like men. I saw many blonde girls too: 'Why are they blonde? Why aren't they dark like me? Because there is less sun? When it's warmer they'll become dark and their hair will be curly? Oh! She put on short sleeves. Look over there, those two women are laughing! Where I come from a woman never laughs with another woman, and no woman would ever wear short sleeves. And they have shoes!' I was startled by all of this.

I remember the first time I went into the city, alone with Edmond Kaiser. Jacqueline had left on another mission. I saw women sitting in restaurants, smoking cigarettes, with their arms uncovered showing beautiful white skin. There seemed to be only blondes with white skin. They fascinated me and I wondered where they had come from. In my country, blondes are so rare that the men covet them, so I thought these girls might be in danger. Edmond Kaiser gave me my first geography lesson: 'These women were born blonde, but others are born different colours in other countries. Here, in Europe, there are also brunettes and red-haired women with little brown marks on their faces.'

'Marks like I have?'

'No, not marks from burns like you. Little

brown spots caused by the sun on their white skin.'

I kept looking for a woman like me, and I often said to Edmond Kaiser, 'May God forgive me, but I would really like to meet another woman who has been burned. I have never seen one. Why am I the only woman who has been burned?' Even today I still feel as though I am the only burned woman in the world. All my life I will feel different. I will always have to conceal my scars under long sleeves. I dream of being able to wear open-necked blouses and short sleeves like other women, but I have to wear clothes that button to the neck. Although I am able to walk about freely, I am a prisoner in my skin.

One day I asked if I could have a shiny gold tooth, something I had always wanted. Edmond Kaiser smiled and said I should first get better and then we could talk about my teeth. In my village, a gold tooth was very special. All that shines is marvellous. I must have surprised him with this strange request, because I had nothing of my own and spent most of my time in bed.

From time to time they took me for walks between treatments but it was weeks before I could have a shower. There was no question of getting dressed before the scars healed. I wore a large loose shirt that covered my bandages. I couldn't read because I didn't know how. I couldn't speak because the nurses didn't understand me, although Jacqueline had left them cards with words written in French and phonetically in Arabic for 'eat', 'sleep', 'bathroom', 'bad', 'not bad', everything that might be useful to them when they were with me. When I could get up, I would often sit by the window. I watched the city, the lights and the mountain above. It was magnificent. I contemplated this spectacle with awe. I wanted to go out and walk. I had never seen anything like it and it was all so beautiful.

Every morning, I went to see Marouan. I had to leave my building to get to the nursery. I was cold since I was wearing only a hospital gown, which closed at the back, a hospital dressing-gown, and hospital slippers. These, and the hospital toothbrush, were my only possessions. I walked quickly, as I did at home, with my head down. The nurse told me to take it slowly but I didn't want to. I wanted to wear a proud look outside because I was alive, even though I was still afraid. That was something the doctors and nurses couldn't do anything about. I felt humiliation and guilt, and I couldn't get rid of them.

At night I often had nightmares, and the face of my brother-in-law would come back to me. I felt him move around me, I heard him saying: 'I'm going to take care of you.' And then I was running in flames. I thought about this during the day, too, and suddenly I would feel the urge to die, to make the suffering stop. Sometimes, lying in my bed, I would think that I should have died because I deserved to. When Jacqueline took me from the hospital to the aeroplane for Switzerland, I believed I was no better than a bag of rubbish that she should have thrown away. This notion, the shame of being what I was, recurred regularly.

Gradually I began to forget my first life. I wanted to be someone else now, to be like the free women I saw all around me and to fit in there as fast as I could. To achieve this, I buried memories of my village and my family. But there was always Marouan, and the nurses taught me how to give him his bottle, how to change him, so that I could be a mother to him for a few minutes each day. I hope my son can forgive me now, but it was difficult to do what was asked of me, because, unconsciously, I felt guilty that I was his mother. Who could understand this? I was incapable of embracing him as my son, of imagining his future with me and my scars. How would I tell him, later, that his father was a coward? How could I prevent Marouan feeling guilty for what I had become – a mutilated body, frightful to look at? I couldn't picture myself 'before'. Had I been pretty, with soft skin, supple arms and seductive breasts? There were mirrors in the eyes of others and I saw myself as ugly, worthy only of scorn.

While my body was being treated and I regained my physical strength, things were not always well in my mind. I did not know how to express this, or the word 'depression'. I became acquainted with it some years later. At the time, I just thought that I should not feel sorry for myself and buried almost twenty years of my life. I think this was necessary for me to survive.

For long months there were skin grafts, twenty-four operations in all. My legs, which hadn't been burned, provided replacement skin until there was none left to give. The grafted skin was fragile and I had to soften and hydrate it. Today I still have to do that.

Eventually Edmond Kaiser decided I should start wearing real clothes. He took me to a department store that was so large and so full of shoes and clothes that I did not know where to look. For shoes, I didn't want embroidered slippers like some women wore at home. And I wanted real trousers, not a *saroual*. I had seen girls wearing them when I went in the van with my father to take the fruit and vegetables to market. In my country some girls had worn trousers that were wide at the bottom, called 'Charleston' trousers. They were considered bad girls, and I wasn't allowed to wear such things.

I didn't get my Charlestons. He bought me a

pair of black shoes with little heels, jeans and a
pretty pullover. I was disappointed. I had been
dreaming of those trousers for nine months. But
I smiled and said thank you. I had got into the
habit of smiling at people all the time and saying
thank you for everything. Smiling was my
response to kindness, but for a long time it was
my only means of communicating. If I cried, I
hid it, an old habit. To smile was the sign of a
new life. Here people were smiling, even the
men. I wanted to smile as much as possible. And
having people say thank you to me was a new
experience. No one had ever said it to me
before, not my father, my brother, or anyone,
when I worked like a slave. I was used to being
hit, not thanked.

I realized that saying thank you was an act of
politeness and respect and it gave me pleasure to
say it because others said it to me. Thank you
for the bandages, the sleeping pill, the cream to
stop me tearing off my skin, for the meal, and
especially for the chocolate. It's so good, so
comforting. I said thank you to Edmond Kaiser
for the trousers, the shoes and the pullover.

'You're a free woman here, Souad, and you can do what you want to do, but I advise you to dress simply, in clothes that suit you, that don't irritate your skin and that don't draw attention to you.'

He was right. In this country that had welcomed me with so much kindness, I was still a little shepherd from the West Bank, without any training, education or family. Who was still dreaming of a gold tooth.

At the end of the first year after my arrival, I left the hospital for a shelter. There were more skin grafts, for which I returned to the hospital. I was learning French, expressions, bits of sentences that I repeated like a parrot, without knowing what they meant. Later Jacqueline explained to me that when she brought me to Europe, it was more important to save my skin than to send me to college, and my hospital stays did not allow for regular French courses. I hadn't even thought about school: in my village only two girls took the bus to school in the city, and people made fun of them. I ridiculed them too, convinced as my sisters were that they would never find a husband if they were educated. Secretly, though, my greatest shame was that I still had no husband. I retained the beliefs of my village: they were ingrained in me. And I told myself that no man would want anything to do with me. For a woman in my country, living without a man is a punishment for life.

In the shelter that had welcomed Marouan and me, everyone thought I would get used to my double punishment of being repulsive to look at and no longer desirable in a man's eyes. They also thought that once I could work I would be able to take care of my son and raise him. Only Jacqueline realized that I was incapable of this, because it would take me years to become a human being again and to accept myself as I was. During those years, because my attitudes were so fixed in what I had learnt in the past, the child would grow up in the wrong way. Also, despite my twenty years, I was still basically a child myself. I knew nothing of life and responsibility, and certainly nothing of independence.

It was at that time that we left Switzerland. My treatment had ended and I could now live elsewhere. Jacqueline found me a foster family, who eventually became my adoptive parents. I loved them and called them Papa and Mama, as did Marouan and the other children. They took in many from all over the world – at one time there were eighteen of us around the table, for the most part abandoned children. These amazing people received from Terre des Hommes the money they needed to shelter the children, and when the children left, it was always painful. I saw some throw themselves into the arms of Papa and Mama because they didn't want to leave them. For many this house was only a temporary home, intended to give them a chance to heal. Some stayed before and after an operation they would not have been able to have in their own country, and then they returned home.

The older ones were expected to take care of the smaller ones, and I helped out as best I could. But one day Mama told me I was paying too much attention to Marouan and not enough

MAROUAN

Marouan was five years old when I signed the papers that allowed our foster-parents to adopt him. I had made some progress in their language – I still didn't know how to read or write, but I could function. It was not abandonment: my foster-parents were going to raise him in the best way possible. In becoming their son, he was going to benefit from a real education, and bear a name that would protect him from my past. I was incapable of caring for him, of providing him with equilibrium or even normal schooling. Many years later, I feel guilty for making this choice, but the years have permitted me to construct a life that then I did not believe was possible – but hoped for. I don't know how to explain these things very well, at least not without breaking down in tears. All these years, I have wanted to convince myself that I hadn't suffered by the separation – but no one can forget their child, and I certainly could not forget Marouan.

I knew he was happy, and that he knew I was alive. At the age of five, how could he not know he had a mother? We had lived together in his adoptive parents' house. But I didn't know how they had explained my departure.

Many of the children in my foster-family had a real family and a country of their own. Those who had nowhere to go, like Marouan and me, were adopted. In the West Bank I was legally dead, and Marouan didn't exist. He was born in Switzerland, just as I was, on 20 December, the day we arrived. And his parents were also mine. It was a strange situation, and when I left that family's home, after almost four years there, I thought of myself almost as Marouan's big sister. I was twenty-four and I couldn't stay there any longer. I had to work, gain my be good for him. When they had talked to me about adoption, they suggested other families might take him, but I refused. 'No, not another family! Marouan will stay here or nothing. I lived with you, I know how he'll be raised here. I don't want him to be placed in another family.' Papa gave me his word. Although I was twenty-four my mental age was probably not quite fifteen. Too much suffering had kept me stuck in childhood. My son was part of a life that I had to forget so that I could build another. At the time, I couldn't understand this clearly. I went from day to day as if I was in a fog, feeling my way along. But I was certain of one thing: that my son had a right to normal parents and a safe life, and that I was not a normal mother. I hated myself, I wept over my burns, my disfigured skin, which condemned me for life. At the beginning, in the hospital, I believed that all these wonderful people could give me back my unmarked skin. When I realized that they could not, I retreated deep inside myself. I was ugly, I had to conceal myself so as not to upset people by my appearance. In the years that followed, as

I acquired a taste for life little by little, I wanted to forget Marouan: I was certain he was more fortunate than I. He was going to school, he had parents, brothers, a sister, and he should be happy. But he was always there, hidden away in a corner of my mind.

If I closed my eyes, there he was. I would see myself running in the street and he was there, too, behind me, in front of or next to me, as if I was running away and he was chasing me. I always had this image of the child that a nurse placed on my knees, the child I couldn't take in my arms, because of the garden where I ran in flames, and my child burning with me. A child whose father didn't want him, who knew that he was condemning us both to death. And I had loved this man and hoped for so much from him! I was afraid that I would not find another man, because of my scars, my face, my body, and what I was inside. I felt I was worth nothing, and I feared seeing people look away.

I began by working on a farm and then, thanks to Papa, I was hired by a factory that made precision tools. The work was clean, and

I was well paid. I checked printed circuits, parts of mechanisms. There was another interesting area of the factory but you had to work on a computer and I didn't feel able to do that. I turned down training for this position, pretending that I preferred to work standing on the line rather than sitting down. One day the head of the team called me: 'Souad? Come with me, please.'

'Yes, ma'am.'

'Sit down next to me. Hold this mouse. I'm going to show you how to do it.'

'But I've never done this, I don't know how. I prefer the line—'

'And if one day there's no more work on the lines? Then what? Nothing at all? No more work for Souad?'

I didn't dare refuse. But I was afraid. Every time I had to learn something new, my hands were damp and my legs trembled, but I gritted my teeth. Every day, every hour of my life, I had to learn new things. I couldn't read or write like the others, and I knew next to nothing of the world. But I wanted so much to work that this woman could have told me to put my head in a bucket and stop breathing and I would have done it. So I learnt how to use a mouse and to understand a computer screen. A few days later, I could do it, and they were all very pleased with me.

I never missed a minute of work in three years. My work station was always impeccable because I cleaned it before I left every day. I was always on time, always there before the others. They had trained me in my childhood with a stick to work hard and to be obedient, to exactitude and cleanliness. It was second nature, the only thing that stayed with me of my former life. I would say to myself that if someone came by unexpectedly I wouldn't want them to find the place dirty. I became a little obsessive about order and cleanliness. If you take an object from its place, you should put it back when you have finished with it. You take a shower every day and change your underwear, you wash your hair twice a week and keep your nails clean. I still look for purity everywhere – it's very important to me. I especially like selecting my clothes, but I know this is because choice was forbidden me in my former life. I like red, for example, because my mother used to say, 'Here's your dress. Put it on,' and it was always grey, ugly, but even if I didn't like it, I had to put it on. So I love red, green, blue, yellow, black, maroon, all the colours I could never have then. I don't have much choice about the style of my clothes. Rolled collar, or high neck-line, buttoned-up tailored shirt, trousers. And my hair has to be over my ears.

Sometimes, in those days, I would sit on a café terrace, bundled up in layers of clothes, winter and summer, and watch the people pass by, the women in mini-skirts or low necklines, arms and legs exposed to the gaze of men. I watched for a man who might look at me but I never found one.

Until the day when I saw from the window of my room a car with a man inside it. I could only see his hands and knees but I fell in love. He was the only man in the world. I saw only him, because of the car, and his two hands on the steering-wheel. I didn't fall in love with him because he was handsome, kind, tender, because he didn't hit me or because I was safe with him, I fell in love because he drove a car. Just seeing it parking in front of the apartment building made my heart beat fast. When I saw him get into and out of it as he left for work or returned, I wept over him. I was afraid in the morning that he wouldn't come back at night.

For a long time I didn't realize that the scene was the same as it had been the first time – later someone had to draw it to my attention. A car, a man who leaves and comes back in it under my window, a man I was in love with before I had spoken to him, a man I spied on while fearing that the car might not return. At the time, I hadn't examined those feelings. Sometimes I tried to work through my memories, to know the reason why certain things happened to me, but I soon stopped. It was too complicated and painful.

Antonio had a red car. I watched until it disappeared from view, then closed the window. I met him, I spoke to him. I knew he had a girlfriend, and I knew her too. And then I waited.

At first, we became friends. Almost three years went by before the friendship turned into something else. I was in love, but I wasn't sure what he thought of me and I didn't dare ask him. I did everything possible to make him love me, to keep him. I wanted to give him everything, to serve him, to spoil him, to feed him. I couldn't see any other way. How could I seduce him? With my beautiful eyes? My shapely legs? My lovely bosom?

First we lived together, without getting married, and it was some time before I was comfortable with him. I couldn't have a light on when I was getting undressed. In the morning, I shut myself into the bathroom as fast as possible, and I would only appear covered in a robe from head to foot. Even now it bothers me to undress in the light because I know my scars are unattractive.

Our first apartment was a studio in the city. We both worked and made a good living. I waited for him to ask me to marry him, but he didn't. I dreamed of a ring and a ceremony, and all the while I did for Antonio what my mother did for my father, what all the women of my village did for their husbands. I would get up at five o'clock in the morning to wash his feet and hair, to lay out his clean, well-pressed clothes. Then I watched him leave for work with a wave, a kiss blown through the window. In the evening, I would wait for him with the meal ready, sometimes until twelve-thirty at night or one o'clock in the morning so that I could eat with him. Even when I was very hungry, I waited for him as the women did at home. The difference was that I had chosen this man and I loved him. No one had forced him on me. I'm sure it was rather surprising to him, a Western man: he was not used to such devotion. In the beginning he would say to me, 'This is great! Thank you, it saves me time, and I don't have to worry about anything.' He was happy. When he came home in the evening, he would sit in his armchair and I would remove his shoes and socks. Then I would give him his slippers. I put myself entirely at his service to keep him at home. I was so afraid every day that he would meet another woman. Then when he returned

we could move from a studio into a larger apartment. He wanted a child, too. It was my first marriage, my first wedding outfit, my first beautiful shoes. A long leather skirt and leather blouse, a leather jacket, and high-heeled shoes! Everything was white leather! Leather is so supple, and it is expensive. I loved the sensation of it on my skin. When I walked through clothes shops, I could never pass a leather garment without touching it, patting it, judging its softness. I had never understood why, but now I know: it was as though I was changing my own skin for a soft, smooth one.

My marriage was the joy of my life. The only thing close to joy I had known until then was my first rendezvous with Marouan's father. But I no longer thought about that. It was forgotten, buried in a mind that was no longer my own. When I became pregnant, I was in Paradise.

Laetitia was a child who was truly wanted. I spoke to her every day she was in my womb. To show off my pregnancy, I wore tight, form-fitting clothes. I wanted the world to see my wedding ring and to know that I was expecting a child. This was the opposite of what I had experienced the first time, but I didn't realize that then. When I was pregnant with Marouan, I'd had to hide myself, to lie, to plead to be married so that a child would not be born to shame my family. Now I was alive and free to walk in public with this new child. I thought I had erased the past with my new happiness. I believed it because I wanted it with all my strength.

Marouan remained hidden in a corner of my mind. One day, perhaps, I'd be capable of facing him and telling him everything. But not yet: I hadn't been completely reborn.

Laetitia arrived like a flower. I had just time to tell the doctor I thought I needed to go to the lavatory when he said I couldn't because the baby was coming. A little flower with black hair and a smooth complexion, she slipped out of me with remarkable ease. Everyone around me said this was exceptional for a first child, that it is rare to give birth so easily. But, of course, she was not my first child. I nursed Laetitia until she was seven and a half months old, and she was an easy baby. She ate everything, she slept well, never had a health problem.

Two years later, I wanted another child. Boy or girl, it didn't matter. I wanted it so badly that it didn't happen. The doctor advised Antonio and me to take a holiday, stop thinking about it and trying so hard. But I was watchful, and I would cry at each disappointment. Finally, I conceived another little girl and we were both wild with joy at Nadia's birth.

She was still quite small when Laetitia, stroking my hand, asked me, 'What is that, mama? A booboo?'

'Yes, Mama has a booboo, but I'll explain it when you're older.'

She didn't mention it again and, little by little, I raised my sleeves to let more of myself show. I did this gradually, not wanting to frighten her. She must have been five when she touched my arm and asked, 'What is that, Mama?'

'Mama was burned.'

'What burned you?'

'It was someone.'

'He was very bad!'

'Yes, he was very bad.'

'Can Papa do to him what he did to you?'

'No, your papa can't because it all happened far away, in the country where I was born, and a long time ago. I'll explain it when you're older.'

'But what did he burn you with?'

'In that country, they didn't have washing-machines like we have, so Mama would make a fire to do the laundry.'

'How did you make the fire?'

'You remember when we went with Papa to get wood in the forest and we made a fire to grill the sausages? I did the same thing. I had a place for making a fire to heat the water. And while I was doing the washing, a man came and he took a very dangerous liquid, which burns everything – it can even burn down a whole house – and he emptied it on my hair and he lit a match and it caught fire. That's how Mama was burned.'

'He's a bad man! I hate him! I'm going to kill him!'

'But you can't kill him, Laetitia. Perhaps God

has already punished him for what he did to me. It was a long time ago and I'm happy now because I'm with your papa and with you. And you know I love you.'

'Mama, why did he do that?'

'It's a very long story and difficult to explain and you're too young to understand.'

'But I want to know!'

'No, Laetitia. Mama has told you she will explain it to you one day. What Mama has just said is enough for now.'

That same day, after the evening meal, I was in an armchair and she was standing near me. She stroked my hair and raised my sweater. I knew what she wanted and it made me uneasy.

'What are you doing, Laetitia?'

'I want to see your back, Mama.'

I let her look.

'Ah, Mama, your skin isn't soft like mine.'

'Your skin is very soft because it's your real skin, but Mama's skin isn't like that because there is a big scar. That's why you have to be so careful with matches. They're only for lighting Papa's cigarettes. If you touch them you can get burned like Mama. You must promise me that you will be very careful. Fire can kill.'

'Are you afraid of fire, Mama?'

I couldn't hide it: it would well up in me at the least provocation. And matches were the worst. It's always been like that.

After this, Laetitia began to have nightmares and I would hear her thrashing about in her bed, shouting for me and clutching her coverlet with all her strength. Once she even fell out of bed. I hoped that things would calm down, but one day she told me that at night she sometimes came to my bed to make sure I was asleep and not dead. I took her to my doctor because I was worried about her and angry with myself for telling her too much. The doctor told me I had been right to tell her the truth, but that I should pay close attention to her from now on.

And then it was Nadia's turn, at more or less the same age. But she reacted differently: she did not have nightmares and she wasn't afraid for me. But I could tell that all was not well: it was clear that she kept everything to herself. For instance, we would be sitting together and she

would sigh. When I'd ask why, she would say,
'I don't know, I just am.'

'The heart that sighs does not have what it
wants. What do you want to say to Mama that
you feel you can't say?'

She surprised me when she said, 'Your ears
are so little. Do you have little ears because you
didn't eat enough?'

'No, sweetheart. Mama has little ears because
she was burned.'

I explained to Nadia in the same way I had
explained to Laetitia because I wanted both of
my girls to hear the same thing, the same words.
So I used the same language, the same truth
with Nadia. It affected her deeply. Nadia didn't
say, as her sister had, that she wanted to kill the
person who had done it, she asked to touch my
ears. I was wearing earrings, which I often do to
hide what remains of my ears.

'You can touch them but please don't pull the
earring because that hurts.'

She touched my ears very gently, then went
into her room and closed the door.

I think that the most difficult thing for the

girls must have been school. They were getting older and Antonio couldn't always pick them up so I had to. I imagined the other children's questions. Why is your mama like that? What's the matter with her? Why does she always wear a sweater in summer? Why doesn't she have any ears?

The next phase of explanations was harder. I simplified it, without mentioning Marouan. I told them that I had met a man, and we loved each other, but my parents would not allow this. They had decided I had to be burned and die because that was the custom in my country when a girl disobeyed her parents. But the special lady, Jacqueline – whom Laetitia and Nadia both knew – had brought me to Europe to be healed.

Laetitia was always the vengeful one, and Nadia was quiet. When Laetitia was about twelve she told me she wanted to go to my village and kill them all. They were almost the same words as her father had used when I told him my story and about Marouan's birth: 'I hope they all die for what they did to you.'

Suddenly my own nightmares returned. I'd be in bed asleep and my mother would appear with a shining knife in her hand. She would brandish it over my head as she said: 'I'm going to kill you with this knife!' And the knife shone like a light and my mother was very real, standing over me. I would wake in terror, sweating, at the moment when the knife shone brightest. The most unbearable part was seeing my mother. More than death, more than the fire, her face haunts me. She wanted to kill me, as she had killed several of her babies. She was capable of anything – and this was my mother, the woman who had given birth to me.

I decided to have one more operation: to deliver me from a physical resemblance to my mother that I could no longer bear to see when I looked in the mirror. I had a little bump between my eyebrows above the bridge of my nose just as she did. I no longer have it, and I think I'm more attractive without it. But after the surgery, the nightmare continued to haunt me. The surgeon couldn't do anything about nursery school, and to write my name. I had to learn the alphabet, letter by letter, at the same time as I was learning to speak the language.

At the end of those three months, I could make out a few words in the newspaper. I began by reading the horoscopes because someone had told me I was Gemini, and every day I slowly deciphered my future. I didn't always understand what I was reading. In the beginning I needed short texts and sentences. An entire article was beyond me. The death notices were a good example of short texts. Nobody pored over them as carefully as I did! 'The X family regrets to inform of the death of Madame X. May she rest in peace.' I also read the marriage announcements and advertisements for used cars, but I soon gave up on those because abbreviated words were too hard for me. Instead, every day, before I went to work, I went into town, had some coffee and read the paper. I loved that time of my day. For me it was the best way to learn. And little by little, when people around me talked about some event, I could show that I knew about it, too, because

I had read about it in the paper. Now I was beginning to take part in conversation.

I know a little about European geography now, the capital cities and some smaller ones. In Italy I've seen Rome, Venice and Portofino, and I visited Barcelona in Spain with my adoptive parents during a summer holiday. I stayed only five days and I remember it being very hot. Also I felt I was depriving Papa and Mama of the beach – they had to stay inside with me, so I went home and they stayed on. It is still hard for me to imagine myself wearing a bathing suit in public. I would have to be alone on the beach as I am when I am undressed in my bathroom.

I have seen a little of the world, and I know that it is a round ball but I've never been taught to understand it. For example, I know that the United States is also America, but I don't know where it is on the ball. I don't even know how to locate the West Bank, my former country, on a map. When I open my daughters' geography books, I don't know where to begin to look for all the countries. Part of the problem is that I have no understanding of distances. If someone like night and day, like wool and silk. That was what I was taught. The Jews were the wool and we Muslims were the silk. That was the only way of thinking. When you saw a Jew in the street, and you almost never saw them anywhere else, fights broke out: stones and pieces of wood were thrown. We were forbidden to speak to them because if we did, we would become Jewish too. But the Jewish people never did me any harm and now I know once and for all that this was nonsense. There is a very nice Jewish butcher's shop in my neighbourhood and the meat there is better than I can get elsewhere. But I dare not go in alone to buy it because of this lingering fear. So I go to the Tunisian butcher because he is Tunisian, not Jewish. I don't know why. I often tell myself: 'Souad, you're going to go there and buy this fine meat. It's meat like any other.' I know I'll be able to do it one day but I'm still afraid. I was told too often at my childhood home to ignore Jews as if they didn't exist. It was more than hatred: they were the Muslims' worst enemy.

I was born Muslim, and while I am still

Muslim and I believe in God, I retain few of the customs of my village. I detest violence. If someone reproaches me for being critical of the Muslim religion by speaking badly of the men of my country – and this has happened – instead of arguing, I try to persuade the other person to listen to me by discussing the issue calmly. I want to help them understand what they haven't understood before. My mother frequently quarrelled with our neighbours. She would throw stones at them, or she would pull their hair. In our country, the women always go for the hair. When she did that I hid behind the door, or in the stable with the sheep because it upset me and I didn't want to see it.

I would like to learn about everything I don't know, and come to a greater understanding of the world. I hope my children will profit from the opportunities they have here. My own misfortune is responsible for their chances. Destiny has preserved them from the violence of my country, from the throwing of stones and the evil actions of men. I want them to have none of the wrong ideas that were put into my head and that I have had so much difficulty getting rid of. I realize now that if I had been told I had blue eyes and I had never seen myself in a mirror, all my life I would have believed I had blue eyes. The mirror represents culture, education, knowledge of oneself and others. Now if I look at myself in a mirror, I think: How small you are! Without a mirror I wouldn't know this unless I walked next to a tall person.

I have realized that I know nothing about the Jews and their history, and if I continue like this I will convey the idea to my children that the Jew is a *halouf*. I will have passed on to them ignorance, instead of knowledge and the ability to think for themselves.

Out of the blue one day, Antonio told Laetitia that he didn't want her to marry an Arab.

'Why, Papa? An Arab is like you, like any other person, like everybody.'

I said to my husband: 'She can marry an Arab, a Jew, a Spaniard, an Italian. The most important thing is that she chooses the person she loves and that she is happy, because I haven't been.'

I love Antonio but I don't know why he loves me and I have never had the courage to ask him, or to say to him: 'Look at me. With all these scars, how is it that you want me when there are plenty of other women?' When I'm talking to him on the telephone, I always ask the same question: 'Where are you, sweetheart?' And when he tells me that he's at home, I am so relieved. I always have inside me this fear of abandonment, a fear that he doesn't love me any more, that I'll be waiting alone in anguish, as I once waited for Marouan's father. I have dreamed several times that Antonio was with someone else. It was one more nightmare. This began two days after Nadia's birth. In my dream Antonio was with another woman, walking arm in arm with her, and I was saying to Laetitia: 'Quick! Go and get Papa!' I didn't dare go myself. My daughter was pulling on her father's coat and pleading, 'No, Papa! Don't go with her! Come back!' She had to bring him to me, and she was tugging at her father as hard as she could. There was never an ending to this nightmare so I never knew whether Antonio came back. The last time I had it, I woke at about three thirty in the morning and Antonio wasn't in bed. I got up to look for him and saw that he wasn't in his armchair and the television wasn't on. I rushed to the window to see if his car was there, then realized a light was on in his study and that he was working on his accounts.

I want so much to be at peace, to have no more nightmares. But anguish, uncertainty, jealousy, a permanent uneasiness about life are always with me. Something in me is broken but people don't realize it because I always smile to hide it. But when I see an attractive woman, with beautiful hair, beautiful legs and lovely skin, when summer comes, a time for the swimming-pool and light clothes . . .

My wardrobe is full of clothes that button up to the neck. While I have bought things like low-cut dresses or sleeveless blouses, I can only wear them under a jacket, which has to be buttoned to the neck. It is the same every summer. I hate knowing that the pool opens on

6 May and closes on 6 September. I want it always to rain or turn chilly. I'm thinking only of myself. When it's warm, I only go out early in the morning or late in the evening. I watch the weather reports and hear myself saying: 'Well, good, it won't be nice tomorrow.' And the children tell me that's not very nice because they want to go to the pool.

If the temperature goes up to 30° centigrade, I shut myself up in my room, lock the door and cry. When I have the courage to go out wearing my two layers of clothes, the one underneath that I'd like to be seen in, and the one on top that hides me, I wonder if the people I pass know about me or if they're wondering why I'm dressed for cold weather in the middle of summer. I love autumn, winter and spring. I'm lucky to live in a country where there is strong sunlight for only three or four months of the year. I was born in a year-round sunny climate but I could no longer live in one. I have all but forgotten my country and the long hours when the golden sun scorched the earth, and how it turned a pale yellow in the grey sky before it set for the night. I don't want that kind of sun.

Sometimes when I look outside at the swimming-pool, I hate it. It was built for everyone's pleasure, of course, but for me it holds anything but that. It was the pool that set off a dreadful depression. I was forty and it was June, which began unusually warm. I had just come in from shopping, and I was looking out of my window at some women who seemed practically naked in their skimpy swimsuits. One of my neighbours, a very pretty girl, was just coming back from the pool in a bikini, a sarong over her shoulders, her bare-chested boyfriend at her side. I was alone in the apartment, obsessed with the idea that I couldn't do what they were doing. It seemed so unfair because it was so hot. I went to my wardrobe and spread out I don't know how many clothes on the bed. I put something on, but it still didn't feel right. Short sleeves underneath, another shirt on top. It was too hot. I tried a lighter shirt, but it was too transparent. I tried on a mini-skirt, but I couldn't wear it because my legs are scarred when the skin was taken for the grafts. Open neck, short sleeves? I can't wear them because of the scars. Everything I laid out on the bed was 'can't wear it'. By then I was sweating heavily and everything stuck to me.

I lay on the bed and began to sob. I couldn't stand being closed up in the heat any more while everyone else was outside with their skin exposed to the air. I could cry as much as I wanted because I was alone. The girls were still at school, which was across the road from the house. Eventually I looked at myself in the bed-room mirror and thought: Why are you alive? You can't go to the beach with your family. If you go, they won't stay in the water, they'll have to come home because of you. The girls are at school but when they come home they'll want to go to the pool. Happily for them they can, but not you! You can't even go to the swimming-pool restaurant to have coffee or lemonade because you're afraid of being looked at. You're covered up from head to foot as though it were winter. People would think you're crazy! You're alive, but unable to live.

You're just an object locked up in the house.

Too many thoughts were colliding in my head. I went into the bathroom, got out the bottle of sleeping pills that I had bought at the chemist, without prescription, because I had trouble sleeping. I emptied the bottle and counted the pills. There were nineteen left and I swallowed them all. After a few minutes, everything was spinning. I opened the window, and I was crying as I looked out at Laetitia and Nadia's school. I opened the apartment door, and heard myself talking as if I were at the bottom of a well. I intended to go up to the sixth floor and jump from the terrace. I was moving as if I was walking and talking in my sleep.

'What will they do if I die? They love me. I brought them into the world. Why? So they could suffer? It isn't enough to have suffered so much myself? I don't want them to suffer. We leave this life the three of us together or nothing. I can't do this because they need me. Antonio says he's at work but maybe he's at the beach. I don't know where he is. But he knows where I am. I'm at home because it's too hot and I can't go out. I can't dress the way I want. Why did this happen to me? What did I do to God? What did I do here on earth to deserve this?'

I was in the hallway, crying and disoriented, but I went back into the apartment to close the window. Then I went into the hall, to the mail-boxes, to wait for the girls. After that, I don't remember anything until the hospital. I had passed out because of the sleeping pills. They emptied my stomach and the doctor kept me under observation. The next day, I found myself in the psychiatric hospital where I saw a very nice woman. I wanted to smile politely when she came into the room, but I burst into tears. She made me take a tranquillizer. Then she sat down beside me and asked me to tell her why I took the pills and why I wanted to end my life. I explained about the sun, and the fire, the scars, the desire for death, and I began to cry again. I wasn't able to sort out what had gone on in my mind. The swimming-pool, that stupid swimming-pool, had sparked it off. Could I really have wanted to die because of a swimming-pool?

'You know that this is the second time you've escaped death? First at the hands of your brother-in-law, and now your own. I think that's a lot, and if you're not treated it might happen again. But I'm here to help you. Do you want that?'

The answer was yes. I was in therapy with her for a month, and then she sent me to see another psychiatrist once a week on Wednesdays. It was the first time in my life since the fire that I had the chance to talk to someone who was there only to listen. I talked about my parents, my unhappiness, about Marouan . . . It wasn't easy. Sometimes I wanted to stop everything but I forced myself to continue because I knew that when I left the session I always felt better.

After a time, I found this psychiatrist too directive, as if she were telling me to take a right turn to get home when I knew I could only get there by going left. She was behaving like a parent with a child. I was required to see her every Wednesday even though I wanted to go only when I felt like it or needed to. I would have preferred, too, that she asked me questions, talked to me, and looked me in the eye instead of at the wall or at her notes. For a year, I resisted the temptation to run away; I knew I was thinking only of myself, not of Antonio and our daughters.

Although I am better now, it is sometimes painful still. Despair can come over me at any time, but especially in summer. We're going to move away from this swimming-pool. But even though our house will be at the edge of a road, summer will still come. Even in the mountains, or in the desert, there will still be summer.

Sometimes I don't want to get up in the morning, I'd like to die and not suffer any more. I have my family and friends around me. I try hard. But I'm ashamed of myself. If I had been burned or paralysed in an accident, I would see my scars differently: no one would be responsible for them, not even me. But my brother-in-law set fire to me because my father and my mother asked him to. It wasn't destiny or fate that made me as I am. That fire deprived me of my skin, of my very self, for my whole life.

And from time to time the terror comes back. Recently, we were watching a movie on television, a Western, and two men were fighting in a stable. One lit a match and threw it into the hay, between the legs of his adversary, who caught fire and began to run about in flames. I screamed and completely lost control of myself. Antonio said, 'Sweetheart, it's a movie, just a movie,' and turned off the television. He took me in his arms to calm me and repeated, 'It's only the television. It's not real, it's a movie.' But it was too late: I was running with flames all over me. I didn't sleep that night. I have such a terror of fire that I freeze at the sight of the smallest flame. I watch Antonio when he lights a cigarette, I wait for the match to go out or the flame of the cigarette lighter to disappear. I don't watch television much because of this. I'm afraid of seeing someone or something burning. My daughters are sensitive to my fears – when they notice something that might upset me, they turn off the television. Everything is electric in our apartment. I don't want to see fire in the kitchen or anywhere else. One day, a boy was playing with matches in front of me. He put some alcohol on a finger and lit it. His skin didn't burn – it was a trick. I was overcome with both fright and anger: 'You go and do that somewhere else! I've been burned. You don't know what it's like!'

A fire in a fireplace doesn't frighten me, provided I don't go near it. Water doesn't bother me if it's lukewarm. But I'm afraid of everything that's hot. Fire, hot water, a gas oven, burners on a stove, saucepans, electric coffee-makers that are always turned on, the television, which might catch fire, faulty electrical sockets, the vacuum-cleaner, forgotten cigarettes – everything that might start a fire. I have terrorized my daughters: it isn't normal for a fifteen-year-old girl to be forbidden to turn on an electric hotplate but if I'm not around I don't want my daughters to use the stove or boil water. I have to be there to be certain that everything is turned off. Every day before I go to bed I check the hotplates.

I live with this fear night and day. I know I make life difficult for others, that my husband is patient but that even he gets tired sometimes of my terror, that my daughters should be able to hold a saucepan without me trembling. They will have to do it one day.

Another fear came to me when I turned forty: it was the knowledge that Marouan was now a man, that I hadn't seen him in twenty years, but he knew that I was married and that he had sisters. Laetitia and Nadia didn't know they had a brother. This lie weighed on me and I didn't speak of it to anyone. Antonio had known about Marouan from the beginning, but we never spoke about him.

Jacqueline knew, too, but she respected my silence. She had asked me to talk to other women at conferences about the honour crime. I owed it to myself to speak about my life as a burned woman, to bear witness as a survivor. After all these years I was practically the only one who could do it.

And I continued to lie in not revealing Marouan's existence. I persuaded myself that I was still protecting my child from the horror of having been the cause of the crime committed against me. But he was almost a man now. The big question was whether I was protecting Marouan or hiding my guilt at having put him up for adoption. It took me some time to grasp that it was all intertwined. In my village, there aren't any psychiatrists, and the women don't ask themselves such questions. We are only guilty of being women.

As my daughters grew up, the questions became more painful.

'But why did they burn you, Mama?'

'Because I wanted to marry a boy I had chosen and because I was expecting a baby.'

'What happened to the baby? Where is he?'

He stayed there in an orphanage. I couldn't tell them otherwise.

SURVIVING WITNESS

Jacqueline asked me to bear witness in the name of the Surgir Association. She waited until I was emotionally capable, after the depression that had devastated me. I was integrated into my new country and I was safe, with a husband and children. I was better, but I still felt fragile in front of those European women. I was going to speak to them about a world so different from their own, about cruelty that would be inexplicable to them.

I told my story sitting on a platform before a small table with a microphone. Jacqueline was next to me. From the start I threw myself into it. And they asked me questions.

'Why did he burn you?'

'What had you done?'

'He set fire to you because you spoke to a man?'

I never said I was expecting a child. I said that if you were only gossiped about in the village, you might end up with the same punishment as someone who was pregnant. I said nothing about my son, who knew nothing of my past or his. I didn't give my real name: anonymity is a measure of safety. Jacqueline knows of cases where the family found a daughter thousands of kilometres away and murdered her.

A woman in the audience got up and asked: 'Souad, your face is pretty, where are the scars?'

'I knew you would ask me that question. I expected it. I will show you my scars.'

I got up and, in front of everyone, undid my shirt. I was wearing a low-cut blouse and short sleeves underneath. I showed my arms, I showed my back. And that woman started to cry. The few men who were there looked uncomfortable. They felt sorry for me. When I had displayed myself in public I felt like a sideshow freak. But in that situation it didn't bother me because I was bearing witness and I had to make people understand that I was a survivor. I was dying when Jacqueline arrived in that West Bank hospital. I owe her my life, and the work she pursues with Surgir requires a living witness to demonstrate to other people the reality of the honour crime. Most people don't know that such things happen, simply because survivors are few. And because, for their safety, they should not go public. They escaped thanks to the shelters provided in several countries by this organization.

That was my first testimony, and I had been in Europe for about fifteen years. My life had changed. I can take risks that recent victims cannot. The questions I am asked relate to my new life, but also to the condition of women in my country. Once, a man asked me this question. Sometimes I have difficulty expressing myself when I am asked a question about my own experience. When it's about someone else, I find the right words and take off.

'Sir, a woman there has no life. Many girls are

beaten, mistreated, strangled, burned, killed. It's normal for us. My mother wanted to poison me to "finish" my brother-in-law's work, and for her this was a normal part of her world. That's what normal life is for women there. You're beaten up, it's normal, you're burned, it's normal, you're mistreated, it's normal. The cow and the sheep, as my father used to say, are worth more than the women. If you don't want to die, you'd better keep quiet, obey, grovel, be a virgin when you're married, and bear sons. If I had not had an encounter with a man, that is the life I would have led. My children would have become like me, my grandchildren like my children. If I had lived there, I would have become "normal" like my mother, who suffocated her own children. Maybe I would have killed my daughters. I might have let one burn to death. Now I think that it is monstrous – but if I had stayed there, I would have done the same! When I was in the hospital there, dying, I still thought all this was normal. But when I came to Europe, I began to understand that there are countries where it is not acceptable to set women on fire, that girls are valued as much as boys. For me, the world stopped at my village. It was a wonderful place, it was the whole world, and it extended all the way to the market! Beyond the market, there were girls who wore makeup, who wore low-cut short dresses. They were the ones who weren't normal. My family was! We were pure as the sheep's wool, but the others, as soon as you got beyond the market, they were the impure ones!

'Girls couldn't go to school. Why? So they would know nothing of the rest of the world. We were controlled by our parents. Education, information, the law, what we know and believe comes to us only from our parents. What they say, we do. That was why there was no school for us. So that we wouldn't take the bus, we wouldn't dress differently, wouldn't be holding a notebook in our hands, wouldn't be taught to read and write. That's being too intelligent, not good for a girl. My brother was the only son in the middle of a family of girls. He dressed as men do here, like in a big city. He went to the barber, to school, to the movies, he went out as he pleased. Why? Because he had a penis between his legs! He was lucky, he had two sons, but in the end he's not the luckiest. His daughters are the luckiest. They have had the great good fortune not to be born!

'The Surgir Foundation, with Jacqueline, tries to save these girls. But it isn't easy. We're sitting here comfortably, I'm speaking to you and you're listening to me. But women in other countries are suffering! It is for this reason that I bear witness for Surgir about the honour crimes, because they continue. I am alive and I am on my feet, thanks to God, thanks to Edmond Kaiser and thanks to Jacqueline. Surgir is a courageous organization and is working hard to help these girls. I admire the people of Surgir. I don't know how they do it. I would rather bring food and clothing to refugees than do their work. The Surgir people have to mistrust the world. They may speak to a woman who seems pleasant enough but who will denounce them because they want to help and she doesn't agree with them. When Jacqueline arrives in one of those countries, she is obliged to behave as they do, to eat, walk and speak like them. She has to blend into that world, has to remain anonymous.'

'Thank you, Madame.'

In the beginning, I was in despair. I didn't know how I was supposed to speak, and now Jacqueline had to tell me to stop talking. After a while, I could speak quite freely before an audience, but I was afraid of the radio because of the other people in my life – the people I work with, and especially my daughters, who knew some things about my other life but not everything. They were eight and ten when I was first invited to take part in a broadcast. They had friends at school and I wanted them to be discreet if they were asked questions afterwards. Laetitia thought it was great that Mama was going to be on the radio and wanted to come with me. This was reassuring but at the same time a little disturbing. I realized that she and Nadia didn't appreciate the significance of my witnessing as a survivor and that, apart from my scars, they knew almost nothing of my early life. One day when they were older, I would have to tell them everything. I felt sick just thinking about it.

The radio interview was the first time I had spoken to such a large audience. My daughters learnt more of my story from it. After they had listened to it, Laetitia reacted violently. 'You get dressed now, Mama, and get your suitcase. We're going to take a plane and go to your village. We're going to do the same thing to them. We're going to burn them! We're going to take some matches and we're going to burn them just the way they did it to you! I can't stand to see you like this.'

She was treated by a psychiatrist for six months, until she said she didn't want to go back, that I was as good for her as the psychiatrist because she could talk to me about everything. I telephoned the doctor, who thought she needed a few supplementary sessions but that for the time being she should not be forced to see him. 'But if you notice later that she's a bit quiet, depressed, I would like you to bring her back.'

I fear my history weighs heavily on them

now, and will in their future. They're afraid for me, and I'm afraid for them. I waited until they were mature enough to understand everything I had not yet told them: the details of my life, the man I wanted for a husband, Marouan's father. I worried about this revelation particularly. I also wanted to help Laetitia and Nadia not to hate the country I come from, and which is half theirs. But they were ignorant of what goes on there. How could I stop them hating West Bank men? The country is beautiful, but the men are bad. In the West Bank, women fight for legal protection. But men make the laws.

At this very moment women are in prison in certain countries because it is the only way to keep them alive. Even in prison they are not completely safe. But the men who want to kill them are at liberty. The law doesn't punish them, or if it does, their hands are soon free again to slit throats, burn, avenge their so-called honour. If someone came forward in a village, in a neighbourhood, to stop the avengers doing harm, ten others would go after the protestor. If a judge treated an honour crime as murder and

and gone into hiding, with or without a child, virgins or mothers.

I have never met any other burned women. They haven't survived. And still I hide, I cannot use my real name, show my face. I can only speak out. It is the only weapon I have.

Part IV

Jacqueline

SOUAD'S LEGACY

My role today, and in the years to come, is to continue working to save other Souads. It will be a long struggle, and money is needed. Our foundation is called Surgir, which means 'arise', because the right moment must 'arise' to help these women escape death. We work throughout the world, wherever we are needed, in Afghanistan, Morocco, Chad, anywhere that we can help. The wider world has been slow to respond to the atrocities inflicted on women in these parts of the world. It has been reported that more than six thousand honour crimes are committed every year, and behind this figure there are countless suicides and 'accidents'.

In some countries, women are imprisoned when they have the courage to complain, supposedly to save their lives. Some have been there for fifteen years because the only people who can get them out are a father or a brother – the very people who want to kill them. If a father asks for his daughter to be released, the warden will not comply. I know of one or two women who were released and subsequently killed.

In Jordan, and this is only one example, there is a law, as there is in most countries, that murder must be punished by imprisonment. But Articles 97 and 98 specify that judges will be lenient with those found guilty of honour crimes. The penalty is generally six months to two years in prison. The guilty men, sometimes considered heroes, usually do not serve the full sentence. Associations of female lawyers are struggling to have these articles amended, and some others have been changed, but not 97 and 98.

We work with women's groups who, for several years, have initiated programmes aimed at preventing violence against women and assisting those who are victims of violence in their countries. Their work is hard and often dogged with obstacles. But, step by step, things have moved forward. The women of Iran have made progress on the issue of their civil rights. Others in the Middle East have learnt that laws in their country give them rights. Appeals have been submitted to parliaments, and certain laws have been amended.

Little by little, the authorities are recognizing these acts as criminal. Statistics are published in the reports of the Human Rights Commission in Pakistan. In the Middle East, public-health law provides information on the number of known cases, and local associations look into cases of violence and research the historical and current reasons for maintaining these archaic customs. Whether in Pakistan, where the government keeps track of the number of girls and women killed, in the Middle East or in Turkey, these customs, which are blindly passed on, must be ended. In recent years, authorities like the late King Hussein of Jordan and the late

Part V
Souad

MY SON

Laetitia and Nadia were still small when I visited my adoptive parents for the first time since I had left Marouan with them. I feared his reaction if I brought him face to face with his two little sisters. He was an adolescent, I had built a life without him, and I didn't know if he would remember me, if he would hold it against me that I had had him adopted. He might even have no interest in us. When I telephoned to let them know I wanted to visit and mentioned my unease, they said: 'No, no, no problem. Marouan knows about it all. You can come.' When I asked about him, they assured me he was doing well. I saw him just three times in twenty years, and every time I was unhappy afterwards. When I got home I cried. My two daughters met their brother without knowing who he was, although he knew who they were. He gave nothing away, demanded nothing. The visits were exhausting. I could hardly speak to him because I didn't have the strength. On my return after the third visit, Antonio said to me: 'I think it's better if you don't go there any more. You cry all the time, you become depressed and it doesn't serve any purpose. He has his life, parents, a family, friends . . . Let him be. Some day you can explain it all to him, if he asks.'

But I always felt guilty, and especially because no one except Jacqueline and my husband knew I had a son. Was he still my son?

The last time I visited Marouan, he was about fifteen. He played a little with his sisters, but our exchange was limited to a few words: 'Hello, how are things?'

'Fine, and you?'

Almost ten years passed. I thought he had forgotten me, that I no longer had any part in his life now that he was a man. I knew he was working and that he was living in a small apartment with a girlfriend, like all the young people of his age. Laetitia was thirteen and Nadia twelve. I devoted myself to their education and persuaded myself that I had done my duty. In moments of depression, I would say to myself that if I was to continue to survive it was better to forget. I envied people who had had no unhappiness in their childhood, who had no secret, no double life. I wanted to bury my first life and try to be like happy people. But every time I took part in a conference when I had to talk about my nightmare life, my happiness wavered. Antonio saw it clearly, and Jacqueline, too. I was fragile, but I pretended not to be.

One day, Jacqueline said to me: 'You know, you could do a real service to other women if you could write a book about your life.'

'A book? I hardly know how to write.'

'But you can speak.'

I didn't know that you could 'speak' a book. A book is so important. I don't read books, unfortunately. Antonio and my daughters do. I prefer the morning paper. I was so impressed by the idea of myself in a book that I couldn't get it out of my head. As my daughters grew up, I knew that one day I would have to tell them more. If it was all written down in a book, it would be less agonizing than having to tell them everything. Until now, I had only told them what they needed to know to explain my appearance. But one day they would want to know everything, and their questions would be like so many knife thrusts into my heart.

I didn't feel able to rummage in my memory for details of the past. If you want to forget badly enough, you really do forget. The psychiatrist had explained to me that this was normal, a result of shock and suffering. But the most important issue was Marouan. I had been living for so long with a protective lie.

If I agreed to tell my story in a book, I would have to include Marouan. Had I the right to do this?

I said no. I was too afraid. My safety and his were at stake. A book goes everywhere in the world. What if my family were to find me or Marouan? They were capable of it. On the other hand, I wanted to tell my story. Too often I had daydreamed about an impossible vengeance. I saw myself returning to my village, well concealed and protected until I found my brother – it was like a film in my head. I would arrive at his house and I would say: 'Do you remember me, Assad? I am alive. Take a good look at my scars. It was your brother-in-law Hussein who burned me, but here I am. Do you remember our sister, Hanan? What did you do with her? Did you give her to the dogs? And your wife, how is she? Why was I burned on the day she gave birth to your son? I was pregnant. Why did you want to burn my son? Explain to me why you did nothing to help me, you, my only brother.

'I introduce my son, Marouan. He was born two months prematurely in the city hospital, but he is big and handsome, full of life! Look at him!

'And Hussein, has he grown old or is he dead? I hope he's still here, but maimed or paralysed, to see me alive in front of him. I hope he is suffering as much as I suffered!

'And our father and mother, are they dead? Tell me where they are so I can go and curse their graves.'

I often have this dream of vengeance. It makes me violent, like them, and I want to kill, like them! They all believe I'm dead, and I would so much like them to see me alive.

For almost a year, I said no to the book unless I could leave my son out of the story. Jacqueline respected my decision. She thought it was sad, but she understood.

But I did not want to write a book about myself without talking about him, and I couldn't bring myself to arrange a meeting with him to resolve the problem. Life went on, but I was constantly saying to myself: 'Do it! No, don't do it!' But how to approach Marouan? I knew I would have to telephone him one day – just like that, without warning, after all these years – and say: 'Marouan, we have to talk.'

How should I introduce myself? As Mama? How should I behave? Hug him? What if he'd forgotten me? He had a right to, since I had more or less forgotten him. Jacqueline forced me to reflect on something that tormented me even more. 'What would happen if Marouan met one of his sisters one day, she didn't know that he was her brother and fell in love with him? What would you do?'

I had never thought of that possibility. We were only about twenty kilometres apart. Laetitia was nearly fourteen and soon the time for boyfriends would arrive. Nadia would follow. Twenty kilometres was nothing. The world is small. In spite of this awful possibility I still couldn't make up my mind. Another year went by.

Finally things sorted themselves out without me. Marouan telephoned. I was at work and Nadia answered. 'I know your mother,' he said. 'We were together in the same foster family. Can you ask her to call me?'

When I came home, Nadia couldn't find the piece of paper on which she'd written the number. She'd looked everywhere. I was a nervous wreck. You might have thought that

Fate didn't want me to be in contact with Marouan. I didn't know where he was living or where he worked. I could have telephoned his adoptive father to find out but I didn't have the nerve. I was a coward and hated myself for it. It was easier to let Fate take its course than to look at myself in the mirror. But Marouan called again two weeks later, and he was the one to say: 'We need to speak to each other.' We arranged to meet the next day at noon. I was going to face my son, and I dreaded what I knew must be in store for me. In short, the questions would be: 'Why was I adopted when I was five years old? Why didn't you keep me with you? Please explain it to me.'

I wanted to look nice so I had my hair done, put on makeup, dressed simply in jeans and a red blouse with long sleeves and closed neck. We had agreed to meet outside a restaurant in the city.

The street was narrow. He had come from the shopping area and I from the railway station so we couldn't miss each other. Anyway, I knew I would recognize him among thousands. I saw him coming, carrying a green sports bag. In my mind he was still an adolescent but this was a man who was smiling at me. My legs wouldn't support me, my hands were trembling, and my heart pounding as if I was meeting the man of my life, as if it was a love tryst. He was tall so he had to bend down to kiss me, very simply, as if he'd left me the day before.

I returned his kiss. 'You did right to call.'

'I also called two weeks ago and when you didn't call back, I thought: So, there it is, she doesn't want to see me.'

I told him that Nadia had lost the number.

'If I hadn't called again yesterday, would you have rung me?'

'I don't know. I don't think so, no. I didn't dare because of your parents. I know that Mama died . . .'

'Yes, Papa is all alone now, but it's OK. And you?'

He didn't know what to call me. This habit that I had developed all those years ago of calling our foster-parents 'Papa' and 'Mama' didn't help. Who was his mama?

I plunged on: 'You know, Marouan, you can call me Mama, you can call me Souad, you can call me the little one, the big one, you can call me whatever you like. And, if God is willing, we'll get to know each other quickly.'

'Agreed. Let's have lunch and talk.'

We sat down at a table, and I devoured him with my eyes. He resembled his father. Same silhouette, same gait, same expression, but he was different. He also looked a little like my brother but with softer features. He appeared to take life as it comes. He was simple and direct.

'Tell me how you were burned.'

'Do you mean that you don't know, Marouan?'

'No one has ever told me anything.'

I explained and, as I spoke, his expression changed. When I talked about the flames that covered my body, he put down the cigarette he had been going to light. 'I was inside you?'

'Yes, you were in my belly. I gave birth all alone. I didn't feel your arrival because of my burns. I saw you – you were between my legs – but that was all. Afterwards you disappeared.

They took you away from me. They put me in a hospital to die. Then Jacqueline searched for you so she could take us out of the country together by plane. We lived together for nine months in a shelter and then we were placed with Papa and Mama.'

'So your burns were because of me?'

'No, not because of you! Never! It's the custom of our country. The men there make their own laws. The ones to blame are my parents, my brother-in-law, but not you.'

He looked at my scars, my ears, my neck, then placed his hand gently on my arm. I knew that he had guessed the rest, and he didn't ask to see. Was he afraid to ask?

'You don't want to see . . .' I began.

'No. This story already breaks my heart, it would give me more pain. What was my father like? Did he look like me?'

'Yes, the upper part of your face. I haven't seen you walk much, but you hold yourself like him, straight, proud. And the back of your neck, your mouth, and especially your hands, even the nails. He was a little taller, muscular like you.

He was handsome. Earlier when I looked at your shoulders I thought I was seeing your father.'

'That must warm your heart, because you must have loved him.'

'Oh, yes, of course I loved him. He had promised that we would get married, but when he learnt I was pregnant he didn't come back.'

'That's disgusting! To drop you! So, in the end, the scars are because of me.'

'Marouan, no. Never think that. They were because of the men in my country. Later, when you get to know that culture better, you will understand.'

'I'd really like to meet my father one day. Couldn't we go there, the two of us, just to see what it's like, and then visit him? I'd like to see his face. Does he know I exist?'

'It would surprise me if he did. I never saw him again. And there's the war now. No, it's better for both of us not to see him or my family.'

'Is it true that you gave birth at seven months?'

'Yes. I was alone when you arrived and you were very small.'

'What time did it happen?'

'The time? I don't know. It was October the first, they told me later. The important thing is that you were whole, from head to foot.'

'Why didn't you talk to me when you came to visit Mama and Papa?'

'I didn't dare to because they had adopted you. I didn't want to hurt them. They raised you, and did everything they could for you.'

'I remember you. We were in the bedroom once, you gave me a yogurt and one of my teeth fell out and there was blood in the yogurt and I didn't want to eat it but you made me. I remember that.'

'I don't. Did you know that at the time I was taking care of the other children and Mama would tell me I shouldn't spend more time with you than with the others? And we didn't waste food in their house because it was very expensive to care for all the children.'

'When I was fourteen or fifteen, I was really angry with you, you know . . . I was jealous.'

'Jealous of who?'

'Jealous of you. I wanted to be with you all the time.'

'And now? Today?'

'I want to get to know you, I want to know so many things.'

'You don't hold it against me for having other children?'

'It's great to have sisters and I'd like to get to know them, too.' He looked at his watch, and it was time for me to go back to work. 'I wish you didn't have to leave. I'd like to stay here with you.'

'Yes, but I must. Can you come to the house tomorrow?'

'No. It's too soon. I'd rather we saw each other somewhere else.'

'So tomorrow evening, at seven o'clock, same place. I'll bring the girls.'

He seemed happy. I hadn't expected it to be so easy because I'd believed he would hold it against me for having him adopted, that he would despise me. But he hadn't even asked the question. He hugged me, I hugged him back, and we said, 'Goodbye. See you tomorrow.'

And I went back to work, my head buzzing like a beehive. An enormous weight had dropped off my shoulders. I was rid of an anguish that had been eating at me for so long, and that I couldn't admit to. I regretted not having been capable of keeping my son with me. One day I would ask him to forgive me for having left him behind so that I could remake my life. I hadn't been able to think straight at the time – I didn't know what I was doing, nothing was real, I was floating. I should have told him that, and also that even though his father had abandoned both of us, I had loved the man. It wasn't my fault that he had been a coward. I thought I should tell him too: 'Marouan, I was so afraid that I beat my stomach in an attempt to lose you.' I wanted him to forgive me for that, too. I had thought that the blood would come to deliver me – I was ignorant and terrified. Would he understand and forgive me?

I was so overwhelmed that I slept badly. Once again, I saw the flames.

Antonio let me deal with it alone, but he

TO BUILD A HOUSE

The next day, Antonio went out with a friend so that I could be alone with the girls. It was Saturday evening, 16 November 2002, seven o'clock. The dinner was lively. They were laughing at everything. Laetitia was talkative, chattering as usual. Marouan had brought his girlfriend. To my girls, he was still just another of the children I had known in my foster-family.

They hadn't grown up together but yet they seemed at ease with each other. I had worried that the evening would be difficult. Antonio had said before he left: 'Call me if you need me and I'll come and get you.' But I felt fine.

Marouan teased Laetitia. 'Come on, Laetitia, sit next to me.' He pulled her close to him.

She turned to me and whispered, 'He's so nice, Mama! And he's so good-looking!'

'Yes, he is.' I studied their three faces. Marouan resembled Laetitia a little, the top of the forehead, perhaps. Now and then I also saw in him an expression belonging to Nadia, who is more pensive and reserved than her sister. Laetitia always expresses her feelings and her reactions are sometimes too impulsive. She inherited that from her Italian father.

Would they understand? Somehow I still saw them as little children and was over-protective. At Laetitia's age, my mother was already married and pregnant.

Suddenly they were all laughing at a man who was quite drunk. He looked at our table, and yelled to Marouan, 'You're lucky to be with all those women! Four – and I'm alone!'

'I'm going to go over there and smash his face!' Marouan muttered.

'No, stay where you are, please!'

'All right.'

The restaurant owner went over to the other man and remonstrated with him, and the meal ended in laughter.

We accompanied Marouan and his girlfriend to the railway station. He lives in the country, and works at garden and park maintenance. He seems to enjoy it and talked about it a little over dinner. Laetitia and Nadia don't yet have clear plans for their futures. Nadia talks about working in fashion design, Laetitia goes from one idea to another. All three walked in front of me on the way to the railway station. Marouan was in the middle and Laetitia held one of his arms, Nadia the other. It was the first time in their lives that they'd done that. I still hadn't said anything. Marouan whispered with his two sisters as if he'd always known them. I had had little joy in my life before my marriage to Antonio and the birth of my two girls. Marouan was born in suffering, without a father, while they were born into happiness and are their father's treasures. Their lives had been entirely different, but their laughter united them better than I possibly could. I felt proud of them all. That evening I lacked nothing. No more anguish or sadness; only peace of mind.

On the platform at the station, Laetitia said to me: 'I've never felt as comfortable with anyone as with Marouan.'

And Nadia added: 'Me too.'

'I'd like to spend the night at Marouan's with him and his girlfriend. Tomorrow we could have lunch together, then catch the train back!'

'We have to go home, Laetitia, your father's waiting for us.'

'He's so nice, Mama, I really like him. He's nice, he's handsome . . .'

It was Nadia's turn to hang on to me. 'When will we see him again, Mama?'

'Perhaps tomorrow or the next day. I'll arrange it.'

'What's she saying, Nadia?'

'I asked Mama if we could see Marouan again and she said OK for tomorrow. Mama? It's OK?'

'You can count on me. I'll sort it out.'

The train pulled out of the station. I looked at the clock. It was one forty-eight in the morning. Both girls ran after it, blowing kisses. I'll never forget that moment. Since I've lived in Europe, I've become used to watches and clocks, and check the time almost obsessively. My memory of the past fails me so often that I always note the present when it's important to me. The day before, Marouan had wanted to know what time he had been born. He needed anchoring, too. But it would be difficult for me to tell him the details of my past. When I couldn't sleep the previous night I'd gone over and over the night of his birth. I remembered I had seen an electric light in the corridor of that hospital when a doctor had taken my son away. The precise time? That is a Western concept. In my land only the men wear watches, so, for nearly twenty years, I had only the sun and the moon to work out the time. I would tell Marouan that he was born at the hour of the moon.

When we got home I left a message on his mobile phone. He rang back to say he and his girlfriend had got home safely and that he'd see us tomorrow.

The girls went straight to bed. When I went into my room, Antonio was still awake.

'How did it go, sweetheart?'

'Perfect.'

'Have you talked to the girls?'

'No, not yet, but I'm ready to tell them tomorrow. I don't have a reason any more for waiting. They liked him immediately. It was as if they'd always known him.'

'Marouan didn't say anything? He didn't refer to anything?'

'Absolutely nothing. He was terrific. Laetitia became attached to him straight away, Nadia, too. They were hanging on to him. They never behave like that with their friends. Never.'

'Are you nervous?'

I was more curious than nervous. Can brothers and sisters recognize each other just like that? How can it be so evident to them that they're connected?

'Maybe you ought to wait a day or two.'

'No. Tomorrow's Sunday. I'll go to the office cafeteria with the girls because there won't be anyone there, and I'll speak to them calmly. We'll see what God gives us, Antonio.'

After my daughters, there would be others to

tell, the neighbours, my colleagues at the office where I'd worked for some years. My job was to organize small receptions, and my bosses' friendship meant a lot to me. How could I introduce Marouan to them as my son after ten years?

I needed to be alone with my daughters. They would judge their mother on a lie she had maintained for twenty years, and might also see me as a woman they didn't know, as Marouan's mother, who had hidden him all these years. The mother who loved them and protected them. I had often told them that they were the great happiness of my life. How could they understand that Marouan's birth was a nightmare?

The next morning, Sunday, I woke up as usual at about nine o'clock. Laetitia asked if I wanted her to make me some coffee. It's the morning ritual and I always answer, 'Yes, please.' I'm a stickler for politeness and respect. I find that European children are sometimes ill-mannered. The language that the girls hear at school is often vulgar, and Antonio and I won't let them use it with us. Laetitia's been scolded more than once by her father for a sassy response. I only had the education of a slave.

Laetitia brought me coffee and a glass of warm water. She hugged me casually, Nadia, too. The love I receive from them and their father surprises me every day, and I often wonder if I deserve it. What I was about to do was so hard.

'I would like to speak to you about something very important,' I began.

'OK, Mama, we're listening.'

I told them we would go to the office cafeteria to talk.

'But you're not working today! You know, I was thinking again about last night. It was great! Has Marouan rung you yet?'

'We stayed out late. He must be asleep.'

If he weren't her brother, I'd have been worried. The girls talked between themselves, unconcerned about the unusual trip to the office on a Sunday morning.

'Last evening, we had a wonderful time. Is that what you wanted to talk to us about?'

'Wait, first things first. So, last night we had a wonderful time with Marouan. Doesn't that say anything to you? Marouan? That makes you think about what?'

'About a nice boy who lived with your adoptive parents. And he's so good-looking.'

'Is it because of his handsome face or because he's nice to you that you like him?'

'Everything, Mama. He just seems very kind.'

'That's true. Do you remember that I was pregnant when I was burned? I talked to you about that.'

'Yes, you told us.'

'But where do you think that child is?'

They looked into my eyes strangely.

'But he stayed there! In your family!'

'No. You have no idea where this child might be? You've never seen anyone who resembles you, Laetitia, or you, Nadia? Or even me? Someone who might have the same voice, who might walk like me?'

'No, Mama. I promise, no.'

'No, Mama.'

Nadia was happy to repeat what her sister had

said. Laetitia was usually the spokesperson, but yesterday I saw a little trace of jealousy appear in Nadia: Marouan had been laughing more with Laetitia, and paying a little less attention to Nadia. Now she listened to me attentively and didn't take her eyes off me.

'You don't know anyone either, Nadia?'

'No, Mama.'

'Laetitia, you're older, you might remember? You certainly saw him at my adoptive parents' house.'

'Honestly, Mama. No.'

'All right, then. It's Marouan.'

'Oh, my God! Marouan? Who we were with last night?'

And they burst into tears.

'He's our brother, Mama! He was in your stomach!'

'He's your brother, he was in my stomach and I gave birth to him all alone. But I didn't leave him there. He came here with me.'

Now I had to explain the most difficult part, the reason for Marouan's adoption. I picked my words carefully, words the psychiatrist had said.

'Build a new life', 'self-acceptance', 'become a woman again', 'become a mother again . . .'

'You kept this to yourself for twenty years, Mama! Why didn't you tell us sooner?'

'You were much too young and I didn't know how you would react. I decided to tell you when you were older. The same is true of how I got the scars ... and the fire. It's like building a house. You have to put one brick after the other. If one brick isn't firmly positioned, what will happen? The others fall. It's the same thing with this, my sweethearts. I wanted to rebuild my house and I thought that later it would be secure enough for Marouan to enter it. If not, it might collapse. But now he's here. It's for you to choose what's next.'

'He's our brother, Mama. Tell him to come and live with us. Nadia, we have a big brother and I've dreamed of having a big brother, and I always said so – like my friends have. And now I have one. Marouan! Right, Nadia?'

'I'll give him my bed!'

Nadia wouldn't normally give me a piece of chewing-gum! But when a brother pops up out of nowhere, she was ready to give him everything!

That was how the previously unknown big brother came into our home. Soon we would buy a bigger house and there would be a room for him. I was consumed with joy. They were soon talking to each other on the telephone all the time, and I thought it wouldn't be long before they were quarrelling. But Marouan is the girls' big brother and he had soon assumed some authority over them: 'Laetitia, you don't answer your mother in that tone! She asked you to turn down the television, and you should do it! You're lucky to have parents, you must respect them!'

'OK, OK, I'm sorry.'

'I didn't come here to quarrel, but Papa and Mama both work. So, what about this untidy room?'

'But we work hard at school, too. You've done it and you know how hard it is!'

'True, but it's no reason to treat Papa and Mama like that.'

And then Marouan took me aside: 'Mama,

does it bother Antonio if I tell off the girls?'

'No, he's quite happy with it.'

'I'm afraid he might tell me to mind my own business, that they're his daughters.'

But Antonio didn't do that. In fact, he was pleased to relinquish a little of his authority. And the girls listen to their brother rather more often than they do their father or mother. They argue with us, slam doors now and again, but not with Marouan. I hope it lasts. Once Laetitia told me Marouan was getting on her nerves.

'He's right, though,' I said, 'just as your father's right. You do answer back.'

'Why does he say he'll go away if we don't listen to him? And that he didn't come here to have to tell us off?'

'Marouan has been through difficult times that you can't understand. Parents are important to him. A mother is precious when you haven't had your own with you.'

If I could only get rid of the guilt that surfaces all too often. If only I could change my skin.

I told Marouan that, if he agreed, I had decided to put our story into a book. 'It will be like our family album. And a witness against the honour crime.'

'One day, I'll go to your village.'

'Why, Marouan? For vengeance? Blood? You were born in the West Bank but you don't know what the men there are like. I still dream about it. I feel hatred, too. I think it would soothe me to arrive in my village with you and shout at them: "Look, everybody! This is Marouan, my son! We were burned, but we aren't dead! Look how handsome, strong and intelligent he is!"'

'It's my father *I* would like to see! I would like to understand why he left you, especially when he knew what was waiting for you.'

'Perhaps. But you will understand better when it is in a book. I will put into it everything that you still don't know, and what many people in the world don't know about. Because there aren't many survivors. The women who do survive still have to hide – for many years. They have lived in fear and they go on living in fear. I can bear witness for them.'

He asked me if I was afraid, and I admitted I

was a little. I'm especially afraid that my children, and Marouan in particular, will live with the thorn of vengeance that, passed down the generations, will leave a mark in their minds. Marouan, too, must build a house, brick by brick. A book is a good thing for building a house.

I received a letter from my son, written in a nice round hand. He wanted to encourage me to undertake this difficult work. It made me cry one more time:

Mama,
After all this time of living alone, without you, to finally see you again, in spite of everything that has happened, has given me hope for a new life. I think of you and your courage. Thank you for making this book for us. It will bring me, too, courage in life. I love you, Mama.
Your son,
Marouan

I have told the story of my life for the first time by forcing out of my memory the things that were buried deepest. It was more challenging than a public testimony, and more painful than answering the children's questions. I hope that this book will travel in the world, that it will reach the West Bank, and that the men will not burn it.

In our house, it will be displayed in a bookcase. And everything will have been said once and for all. I will have it bound in a pretty leather so that it isn't damaged, and with beautiful gold lettering.

Thank you,

Souad,

Somewhere in Europe.